THE TASTES OF TRAVEL

Elisabeth de Stroumillo

THE TASTES OF TRAVEL

NORMANDY
BRITTANY

Collins and Harvill Press
London, 1979

© 1979 Elisabeth de Stroumillo

ISBN 0 00 262807 4

Made and printed in Great Britain by
William Collins Sons & Co Ltd, Glasgow
for Collins, St James's Place and
Harvill Press, 30A Pavilion Road, London SW1

Contents

Hotels and restaurants mentioned in the text are marked with a star on the area maps.

Foreword

This is in no way a conventional guide-book; it is not scholarly enough. Nor is it a conventional cookery book; it is not comprehensive enough. It is a highly personal attempt to unite, however superficially, the various elements which make travel more than just a progression through a series of geographical, climatic and architectural features; an effort at bringing into focus not just places that please but also the people who have animated those places in the past, and the culinary flavours that are often the most evocative souvenirs after the places have been left far behind.

Being highly personal, it is also rather arbitrary, especially with regard to the way in which I have 'divided' the territory. But I cannot apologise for having left out some places and a great many more people; even if space were no consideration, one cannot have been everywhere nor be interested in everybody who passed that way before.

Not a word, incidentally, was written without a large-scale Michelin map open beside me; consequently it will be easier to follow if the same maps are used in conjunction with the text.

The fact that they tie in neatly with the annual *Red Michelin Hotel and Restaurant Guides* may also be useful to people who are not always following my own itineraries. I have named my personal choices of hotels and restaurants wherever I am reasonably sure that their standards will not fluctuate wildly, but I cannot pretend to have stayed or eaten in every town and village I have visited, nor that places I have liked will never change hands or ambience for other reasons. I tend to prefer small, unpretentious establishments where possible, preferably family-run, and if I have not been steered towards them by some reliable recommendation, I usually start my search near the railway station: modest French restaurants and hotels that cater for the passing trade are almost invariably excellent value.

They do not, however, tend to go in for high-flying gastronomic repertoires, so except in the case of very rarefied establishments whose *specialités* are their hallmark, I have refrained from naming specific dishes. It is a risky thing to do, anyway, when the cook may fall ill or go elsewhere without notice. But I have eaten some highly interesting local dishes simply by looking down the *menu du jour* and asking which is the *specialité régionale*, or *de la maison*, and taking the advice proffered, and I am sure that anyone who follows the same methods will derive equal gastronomic pleasure.

I am eternally grateful to Mrs. Pauline Hallam, of the French Government Tourist Office in London, who has helped me over many an arrangement and on occasion sent out *cris de coeur* to her colleagues in France for reassurance and help over a point of detail or a recipe. I am equally grateful to my family, who have put up uncomplainingly with my insatiable urge always to look round one more corner, and have patiently kept moving with me throughout my peregrinations when they would probably much rather have stayed still, and who have eaten their way enthusiastically through strange concoctions when they would probably much rather have had roast chicken or grilled hamburgers. Great gratitude is also due to *The Daily Telegraph*, under whose benign aegis so much of my travelling is done.

Lastly, a general salute to all those authors, often anonymous, of the truly scholarly guide-books and histories and cookery books and reference books without which one could travel indefinitely yet still remain ignorant, and feast lavishly without discrimination, and upon which I have relied greatly in checking dates and facts; any mistakes are mine and not theirs. And a special salute to Ruth Eve, who turned so many messy pages into neat typescript and interpolated valuable notes and comments in the process.

ELISABETH DE STROUMILLO

PART I

Normandy

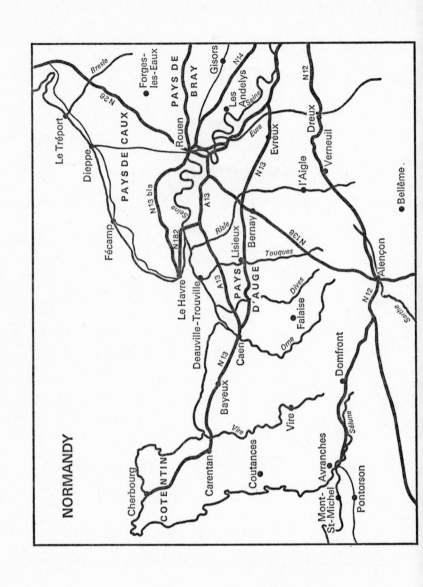

History

Unlike Brittany, which has geological and geographical unity as well as ethnic identity, Normandy is a man-made phenomenon covering a variety of geographical features. To the east are wide, chalky plains shading into pastures and woodlands; to the west, the characteristically rocky Armorican formations of Brittany. And between them, like a cushion, a transitional zone, split into a mosaic of differing regions, or *pays*.

A countryside of enormous diversity, in fact, and one that only emerged as an entity after the 9th century, when the Norse raiders had commandeered and settled it.

Long before that, in pre-Christian times, all the lands west of the Seine were populated by Gauls of Celtic origin whose forebears, during the 3rd century BC, had brought tin from Cornish mines to the foundries of Bronze Age Europe. When the Roman legions swept north in 56 BC, they established their main strongholds along the Seine valley: Rotomagus (Rouen) and Juliobona (Lillebonne). This was their original port, succeeded after it had silted up by another one, due east of it, called Caracotinum, now Harfleur. From these centres they controlled this part of Gaul until the end of the 4th century.

Christianity gradually crept northwards into this Roman province: the first bishopric was founded at Rouen in AD 260 by St. Nicaise, and others soon followed, among them Evreux, Bayeux and Fécamp. The invasion of Clovis, King of the Franks, in the 5th century and the establishment of Neustria, his Kingdom of the West, temporarily shook this placid province, but the Christian faith continued to spread. More dioceses were founded in the 6th and 7th centuries, also the first monasteries, centres of learning and prosperity as well as of religion, notably St. Wandrille (then called Fontenelle) and Jumièges, both on the Seine. And in the West, in 709, Bishop Aubert of Avranches brought the cult of St. Michael to the hilltop that was to become Mont-St. Michel.

Barely a hundred years later, and only two decades after Charlemagne was crowned Emperor of the West, the invasions started that were to make Normandy what it is today. Skilled navigators and ruthless fighters, Vikings from Scandinavia sailed down Europe's western shores, plundering and conquering as they went. The opulent and defenceless towns and monasteries of the Seine valley and the neighbouring coasts were an easy prey. Citizens who at the outset must have come to stare curiously as the first Viking longships beached, were butchered and robbed and, from about 820 for the best part of a century, succeeding waves of Norsemen looted and laid waste more or less as they pleased. They were wily as well as predatory: faced with any resistance they would feign penitence, receive baptism, make peace treaties and then move on, only to be followed by new bands of marauders.

Eventually, there being little left to loot, their belligerence began to abate and they became more tractable, and when King Charles the Simple conceived the idea of turning the raiders into bona fide residents, peace was within sight. At a meeting in 911 between the King (whose nickname, far from indicating stupidity, was a tribute to his straightforwardness) and the Norman leader, Rollo, at St. Clair-sur-Epte, a pact was made whereby the Normans became official settlers of all their captured territory.

The Duchy of Normandy had come into being and Rollo, its first Duke, wasted no time in bringing law and order to it; he proved a born administrator. He had himself baptised, thus regularising his union with Popa, daughter of the Governor of Bayeux, by whom he had already produced an heir, and then proceeded to discipline the other Viking-conquered domains, revitalising agriculture and trade and encouraging his more loyal nobles to build castles and fortresses (few of which, in the 10th and early 11th centuries, were of lasting stone construction).

At the same time, generous reparations were made to the Church for past depredations: during Rollo's twenty-two years of tenure, and under his successors, ruined abbeys and monasteries were restored and new ones founded; art, architecture and learning flourished, and Normandy became one of the most civilised states of the Middle Ages. The earliest, and some of the finest, ecclesiastical buildings that survive, or partly survive, were stone-built in the Romanesque style that was born in Normandy. Not until the end of the 12th century did the French-inspired Gothic style take hold there, and by this time the great stone feudal castle-fortresses were also being built in strategic locations along the borders of the Duchy and within it: massive *châteaux-forts* whose core was the keep, or *donjon*, and whose walled courtyards could contain a garrison.

Little more than a hundred years after Rollo's death, Norman influence also started to spread beyond its territorial borders. Three sons of the Hauteville family from the Cotentin peninsula, chafing under the repressive rule of Rollo's great-great-grandson, Robert the Magnificent (also called Robert the Devil), set off for the holy places of the Mediterranean. Here they and their kinsmen, the Guiscards, carved out princedoms for themselves in Apulia and the Levant and, more importantly, created the brilliant Kingdom of Sicily that was to last for nearly two hundred years; the great Cathedral and cloister of Monreale, above Palermo, is a legacy of this Norman realm.

Even more remarkable than the Hautevilles, the Guiscards, and those later Normans who sailed away to make discoveries in Africa and the New World, however, was Robert the Magnificent's bastard son William, born to a Falaise tanner's daughter in the same year (1028) that his father succeeded to the Duchy. Duke Robert, who was probably a highly unbalanced character, having disciplined the more recalcitrant barons and made them also swear loyalty to his son, abruptly betook himself to the Holy Land and died in Nicaea in 1035. William thus became Duke of Normandy when only seven, and the nobles took this cue to resume their private feuds. Rescued by his mother and her husband, he lived quietly with them until old enough to start regaining his dukedom, a struggle he embarked upon when still not twenty years old and finally accomplished by about 1062. In the course of these activities he also found time to court and marry his cousin, Matilda of Flanders (which put him temporarily out of favour with the Pope).

In January of 1066 William's childless cousin, Edward the Confessor, King of England, died. He had already named William as his heir, but his emissary, Harold, although he duly swore fidelity to William, could not resist, when the time came, taking the English crown for himself. Consequently William, once more morally supported by the Pope, set about mustering military support for his own claim. By some astonishing feat of diplomacy he managed this at a general meeting called at Lillebonne, and by an even more astonishing feat of organisation he then assembled a fleet and an army, arranged for a diversionary Norwegian raid to be made on Northern England, crossed the Channel, landed in Sussex, and had defeated Harold's army at the Battle of Hastings, by the end of September of the same year.

It was William's conquest of England that sparked off the almost endless wars in which that kingdom sought either to retain or enlarge its French territories, or to combat French influence in other parts of the world, and this enmity between the two countries was to last, with few interruptions, for nearly eight centuries. Normandy itself remained an independent Duchy, united with England, until 1204, when King Philippe-Auguste won it, together with Anjou, Maine and Touraine, for France. Early in the following century (1314) the 'Norman Charter' gave Normandy, still nominally a Dukedom, a certain provincial individuality which it was to retain until the Revolution, but in the meantime it continued to be a battleground: for the Anglo-French Hundred Years War (1337-1453) and, to a lesser extent, for the Religious Wars of the 16th century.

Its ducal status virtually lost (though the present Queen of England retains the title of Duke of Normandy), its political significance also dwindled, and its art and architecture followed the same lines as those of the rest of France. But two Normans contributed significantly to French Classicism: the writer, Pierre Corneille, and the painter, Nicolas Poussin.

During the 19th century, several Norman writers (de Maupassant and Flaubert among them) attained international status, and 19th-century French painting is studded with famous Normans like Millet, Boudin and Monet. Thanks partly to their influence Normandy's sea- and landscapes inspired a host of other painters: Impressionists like Sisley, Renoir, Pissarro and Cézanne; Pointillists like Seurat and Signac, and contemporaries like Braque, Léger and Dufy.

When, following the French Revolution in 1789, Normandy was divided into five modern administrative departments of which it still consists, and which do not always correspond with its ancient boundaries, one might suppose its identity to have been forever submerged in rural France. But even had the distinctive Norman character thus been eradicated (which is far from the case) it retained its niche in history through the reverse invasion of June 1944, when the Allied troops stormed its beaches to put an end to the Second World War. The epic battles fought on Norman soil at that time probably left as much devastation behind them as all previous wars put together, particularly in terms of domestic architecture, which for centuries had traditionally been based on timber-framing. But it is very much part of the practical Norman character to waste no time on regrets but to get on instead with renewal, and the new buildings and whole new towns remind one throughout Normandy that this has been done.

This sturdy common sense, which is the core of the Norman temperament, is also an important ingredient in the strongly homogeneous *feel* of Normandy. It is a region where people maintain their traditions, working without fuss to produce fine things that contribute to both physical and visual well-being, like their lovely faïence (going back at least to the 13th century); their fine pure-bred horses; their cider and Calvados (the Norman apple brandy) and cream and butter and ambrosial cheeses, all of which figure so richly on the Norman table.

Specialities

Cream is probably the most omnipresent ingredient in true Norman cuisine, discreetly mingled with the other two 'Cs'—cider and Calvados—in a number of sauces. Any dish described as being *à la Normande* on a menu will undoubtedly contain at least two of these ingredients: fish poached in a cider-laced *fumet*, perhaps, and served with a satiny blanket of sauce which combines the reduced *fumet* with cream and a knob of butter; game or fowl that is flamed in Calvados before roasting and appears with a cream-enriched sauce again based on the cooking-liquid. More often than not, the fish sauces will also be embellished with a few mussels and shrimps and mushrooms, as in *Sole Dieppoise*; likewise fowl and meat are frequently cooked and served with slices of apple. Even if dishes like *Poulet Vallée d'Auge*, *Poulet Cauchois*, and *Poulet Vallée de la Risle* appear somewhat alike, there are always subtle differences that are worth exploring; similarly there are wonderful nuances in the preparation of duckling, a speciality of the Seine valley. Not perhaps quite in the same class, but some of my own favourite Norman dishes nonetheless, are the varieties of chitterlings and sausages—*andouilles*, *andouillettes*, *boudins*—to be found, and the different manners in which they, too, are cooked: never with cream, for they are too rich, but sometimes roasted with apple slices and sometimes split and grilled to crispness. In desserts, apples are used lavishly and delectably: what looks like a totally predictable apple tart will turn out to have a flavour no other apple tart ever aspired to, and Norman chefs have ambrosial ways with pears, too.

But more of food in due course; now for a look at Normandy itself, starting with the wedge-shaped region to the north and east of the Seine.

Pays de Bray
Pays de Caux

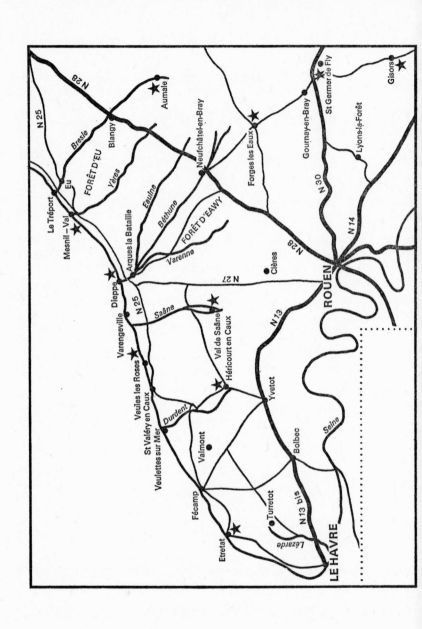

Dieppe, gateway to this part of Normandy and the oldest of the ancient Duchy's three principal ports (it was a Gallo-Roman settlement, and later a Viking base), is also France's longest-established seaside resort: the dashing Duchesse de Berry launched the fashion for sea-bathing here, in 1824. Sitting almost astride an imaginary line drawn between London and Paris, it is equally one of the traditional crossroads for Anglo-French traffic, especially after its link, amid much rejoicing, by a new and largely English-built branch line to the Paris-Rouen-Le Havre railway in 1848. Yet despite its pre-eminence as a port, and despite the sun-hunger that has wooed the mass of holidaymakers away to sultrier beaches, Dieppe is far more than just a clutch of quaysides with a long and underpopulated beach stretching away to the south-west of them. It has a busy and animated inner core that seems oddly divorced from its seafaring activities and is almost a microcosm of provincial Norman town life.

The effect is as though three quite separate places had been nudged together on to one spot, and I find it enormously captivating. Even the port is a mosaic of varied activities; travellers who merely steam into the outer part, disembark at the Gare Maritime and roar off southwards will probably get a glimpse of the fishing port immediately behind the ferry terminal but will miss all the fun of the commercial port, further back again, where huge cargoes of bananas from the West Indies and other fruits and vegetables from Morocco swing across the quaysides, and the air is full of fruity smells and hoarse cries in a mixture of French accents from across the seas. Flanking the fishing and ferry ports are the arcades where barrels of mussels and shrimps stand higgledy-piggledy outside innumerable cafés and solid-looking citizens in *bleu de travail* denims and overalls put away vast platefuls of crustaceans at all hours of the day. Nearby is the modest and excellent *Armorique* restaurant, convenient both for the Gare Maritime and the Quai Duquesne fish market where, in the early morning, fat turbot and brill and sole lie or feebly flap in shining heaps and marketeers and housewives and restaurateurs haggle and gossip raucously.

At right angles to the port, the beautifully landscaped and grassy seafront esplanade which flanks the broad beach seems to belong to another world. Here are the tennis courts, the children's playground, the municipal swimming pool, the Syndicat d'Initiatives and the Casino (with the town's best restaurant). Here too, lined up like a wall of sentinels facing seawards, the more sedate hotels (I particularly like the *Windsor*) cater alike for the remnants of their traditional family clientèle and a mixture of itinerants. And behind them, in the triangle formed by port and resort, is the old town, watched over by the castle from the west and centred on the animated Place du Puits Salé, where the fountain has bubbled up spring water for the past four hundred years and the *Café des Tribunaux* is the traditional place for sitting and watching the comings and goings all around it. Nearby are the Gothic church of St. Jacques with a lovely rose window; the Renaissance St. Rémy; the shops of the Grand Rue and a cobweb of the old streets that on Saturdays are crammed with market stalls and at other times evoke memories of Oscar Wilde in exile, and of the Dieppois composer Saint-Saëns, and of the paintings of Pissarro, Sickert and Braque.

Moving towards the western point of this triangle and past the vestiges of 14th-century fortifications, Les Tourelles, a monument in the Square du Canada recalls the exploits of Dieppois voyagers to the New World between the 16th and 18th centuries. Less eye-catching is the plaque nearby that commemorates the 1942 Allied raid on Dieppe, in which the

Canadian 2nd Division suffered disastrously.

On the cliff top above this end of the town stands the formidable bulk of Dieppe Castle, dating back to the 15th century and housing a museum full of mementoes of the town's past and particularly of its sea-going explorers. Most interesting of all the exhibits, though, is the unique collection of ivory carvings made by Dieppois craftsmen from African elephant tusks brought back by generations of sailors from the Renaissance period onwards. The intricacy of the workmanship is amazing however much one abhors the idea of slaughtering elephants for their ivory, and in this respect it is interesting to discover that the vogue declined as long ago as the late 19th century—due more to the fact that ivory was becoming expensive rather than to concern about the preservation of elephants. One wonders why the carvers did not turn to wood, of which there is so much in the environs of Dieppe; instead, the tradition seems to have died out completely.

Dieppe harbour lies at the mouth of the Arques, a short stretch of river formed by a merging of the Varenne and the Béthune, and the Varenne is the natural frontier line between the humpy, forested farmlands of the Pays de Bray to the south-east and the chalky plains of the Pays de Caux to the west. Strictly speaking, the Bray country stops well short of the coast, but most of the countryside east of Dieppe is a natural extension of it, with the valleys of the Yères and the Eaulne prolonging the gentle green undulations that are its chief characteristic. The Eaulne skirts a patch of ancient forest that once extended over most of the region south-east of Dieppe and on whose edge are the remains of the feudal castle of **Arques-la-Bataille**, looking rather disdainfully down upon the little industrial town below it. Here the Protestant Henri of Navarre, France's beloved Henri IV, repelled with 7,000 men the 30,000-strong Catholic forces of the Duc de Mayenne in 1589. **Envermeu**, on the other side of the Arques forest and bordered by the Eaulne, has an unfinished Gothic church with an attractive, airy chancel and apse.

The stretch of coast on this side of Dieppe is largely uninteresting as far as the mouth of the Yères, which trickles past the nice, slate-covered belfry of St. Martin-le-Gaillard's 13th-century church and meets the sea at the little resort of Criel-Plage. Just beyond it, the slightly larger and prettier resort of **Mesnil-Val** has a charming hotel converted from an old Norman house, the *Vieille Ferme*, with cottages tucked into a flowery garden. Beyond this again the border of Normandy is marked by the river Bresle with **Le Tréport** at its mouth; now a fishing port and small resort, it was in 1066 the point from which William the Conqueror's fleet finally left the French coast for the invasion of England.

A short distance upstream is the sleepy little town of **Eu**, wrapped around a vast and (architecturally) thoroughly undistinguished château, largely rebuilt after a fire in 1902, standing in a park laid out by Le Nôtre, of Versailles fame. To English visitors it is interesting because Queen Victoria and her consort twice stayed there as guests of Louis-Philippe, in 1843 and 1845; the Queen was enchanted both with the 'dear place' and the 'dear King and Queen' (with whom she continued on the friendliest terms after their exile to England in 1848). In the same year that the French sovereigns fled, John Ruskin crossed the Normandy border at Eu with his young wife Effie, combining his honeymoon with a study-tour of Norman church architecture. They found the château full of pictures of the Royal visits which seem to have deflected Ruskin's attention from its rather awful shape. Had he passed through Eu a few years later, he would probably have had some scathing things to say about Viollet-le-Duc's restoration of the church of Notre-Dame et St. Laurent, opposite the château, for he was the implacable enemy of restorers. Despite the restoration work, however, the huge early Gothic church is particularly harmonious inside and its crypt contains the tomb of St. Lawrence O'Toole, Primate of Ireland, who died there in the 12th century.

The great Forest of Eu unrolls inland, fringing the course of the Bresle, its well-tended glades of huge beeches criss-crossed by a network of little roads and forest paths and broken by patches of open spaces and a few hamlets. Blangy-sur-Bresle, halfway along it, has been almost entirely rebuilt since the Second World War; further up the river the forest starts to peter out and by **Aumale** it has given way to pasturelands. Aumale (with a nice small hotel, the *Dauphin*) is a dairy town, and indeed from here south to Gournay and westward across the Béthune almost to the Forêt d'Eawy, south of Arques, most of this verdant countryside is devoted to supplying Paris with milk, cream, *demi-sel* cream cheeses and the distinctive cylinder-shaped *bondon* cheeses of Neufchâtel. There are a few interesting buildings: the 11th- and 12th-century church of St. Hildevert at Gournay (home of the soft St. Gervais cheeses) and the even more remarkable, very early Gothic abbey church in the hamlet of **St. Germer-de-Fly** just south of it (with a good restaurant, the *Auberge de l'Abbaye*). There's a tall-spired 16th-century church at Argueil, and Notre-Dame at Neufchâtel, and there's a lovely pale early Renaissance château at Mesnières-en-Bray where Henri IV is said to have stayed with his mistress, Gabrielle d'Estrées. Otherwise, with one notable exception, the low-lying Pays de Bray is an utterly rural region of comfortable farmsteads and unassuming villages.

The notable exception is **Forges-les-Eaux**, a tidily manicured and cheerfully sophisticated little spa that has been well patronised by *curistes* since the time of Louis XIII. Nowadays it is equally thronged, especially at weekends, by Parisians who enjoy a flutter at the gambling tables, for it rejoices in the nearest casino to the capital. (Ever since 1919 casinos have been forbidden within a 100-kilometre radius of Paris, and Forges-les-Eaux is lucky to be 19 kilometres, or about 12 miles, outside this limit. The *Casino* restaurant is good, too.)

Due south of the Pays de Bray the river Epte has been the south-eastern border of Normandy for over a thousand years, and the great fortress at **Gisors**, overlooking this river, has stood there for only some one hundred and fifty years fewer. Surrounded by gardens, and a town that was largely rebuilt following the Second World War, it is a magnificently impressive sight. It makes a convenient overnight stop (try the *Hôtel Moderne*, near the station) before going on to follow the Epte as it curls through a charming little valley towards the Seine (dealt with in the next chapter). The pretty riverside road goes past St. Clair-sur-Epte, where the Duchy of Normandy was born of the pact between the Viking leader, Rollo, and King Charles the Simple; past the ruined keep of William Rufus's fortress at Château-sur-Epte, and past the 15th-century bridge at Aveny. Just beyond this a little road winds back north towards the main N14 (less frequented now that the *autoroute* carries the heavy traffic between Paris, Rouen and Le Havre) and a side road off the N14 leads to the great forest of Lyons, studded with some really stupendous old trees. There are also the churches of Lisors and Ménesqueville to see on its southern outskirts, and the ruined Abbey of Mortemer, and, at the heart of the woodland the almost too prettified small town of Lyons-la-Forêt, its colour-washed and timber-framed houses sparkling like new toys.

North-westwards, a nice little road winds towards Vascoeuil and its lovely manor house in the Andelle valley; a little way upstream the ruined castle of L'Héron occupies a pleasant, grassy site where the Héronchelles joins the Andelle. Another small road follows the course of the Héronchelles northwards, past picturesque Yville, leading eventually to the upper Varenne valley and the Eawy forest and thence back towards Dieppe.

One is then back on the edge of the Pays de Caux, but before moving too far north-westwards there is a curious little spot a mere 23 kilometres (about 15 miles) due north of Rouen that belongs neither to the Pays de Bray nor to the Pays de Caux, nor even to the Seine valley but purely to itself and its setting of cushiony fields and tangled lanes: **Clères**. Considering how close it is to Rouen, and considering that it possesses not only a motor museum but also a château with a wildlife park, it is remarkably unspoilt. It is a dear little village, too, with a brook chattering through it, and a minute inn (the *Cheval Noir*) where the food is excellent and the rooms no more than basic – but worth bearing with just for the pleasure of visiting the park when the gates open in the morning, and deer and wallabies peer curiously at early-comers through the damp trees and all sorts of exotic birds lift off the misty surface of the lake and circle on lazy wings just out of arm's reach.

The plain that stretches almost unbroken from the Varenne valley westwards to the upper 'jaw' of the Seine estuary is often thought of as dull and uninteresting. I do not find it so. Most people ignore it in favour of the coast, but I love its openness and the almost golden luminosity of its skies, especially in autumn; and the trees clumped about the farmsteads or spaced in stately procession to give protection from the winds dispel any monotony. Pastures of statuesque cows alternate with fields of crops and orchards; there are unexpected shallow valleys cutting into the chalk; and villages that from the map might appear to be nothing special are frequently highly picturesque, with nice stone-built churches and cottages and the occasional thatched roof whose ridge is protected by a plantation of mosses and ferns and irises. And, as throughout Normandy, there are endless glimpses of lovely half-timbered manor houses and the occasional imposing château.

One such is just south of Dieppe and only a short way west of Arques-la-Bataille: 17th-century Miromesnil, where Guy de Maupassant was born and which is open to the public. Another is nearer the coast to the west of Dieppe, reached from Miromesnil via Offranville, whose 16th-century church has some good glass: this is the Manoir d'Ango. Jean d'Ango was a 16th-century Dieppois shipping magnate who prospered by legalised privateering at a period when the Portuguese were harassing all ships trading with Africa. With the blessing of François I, he created a fleet which sank or captured some three hundred Portuguese ships. His operations were so successful, in fact, that the Portuguese opened negotiations with the French King that eventually put Ango out of business, but by this time he had made a big enough fortune to build himself a mansion in Dieppe itself (which no longer exists), a chapel in Dieppe's St. Jacques church that still houses his tomb, and this well-restored country seat at Varengeville, which is delightful.

Varengeville is a loosely grouped, shady little resort sloping down deep lanes from the main road past well-kept country houses towards the sea; its other claim to fame is a small clifftop church dating back to the 12th century with a brilliant Jesse window designed by the artist Georges Braque, who lies in the tiny churchyard outside. A minute road goes westwards along the cliffs from here to the Ailly lighthouse and then loops back erratically before reaching Ste. Marguerite, with an enchanting small church, originally Romanesque but largely rebuilt in the 16th century. Beyond it, tiny resorts are tucked into occasional breaks in the creamy-coloured cliffs; inland is the great square-based 13th-century tower of Bourg-Dun's Notre-Dame church, and the little valley of the Saane winds up to **Val-de-Saane** and a delightful country restaurant of the same name. **Veules-les-Roses** is a small, pretty resort with a minute, deservedly popular and somewhat expensive restaurant, *Les Galets*; next down the coast comes **St. Valéry-en-Caux**

which, although largely destroyed during the Second World War, nonetheless has enormous charm, with a deep and narrow picture-postcard harbour, a nice pebbly beach, and a general air of wholesome cheerfulness. Henri IV is supposed to have stayed there, in the house that bears his name and is one of the few remaining old buildings, and on the cliff tops to either side of the resort are moving monuments to the French and Scottish troops who fell there during their retreat in 1940.

Veulettes-sur-Mer, the next tiny resort westwards, lies near the mouth of the Durdent, whose valley I find the most charming in this part of Normandy. The small pilgrims' chapel of Notre-Dame de Janville watches over its lower reaches; further upstream, Cany-Barville has a beautifully placed church with a 13th-century belfry, and a splendid Classical château is visible just south of it. There are innumerable old watermills dotted along the course of the stream, and a sweet small hotel, the *Auberge de la Durdent*, just outside the hamlet of **Héricourt-en-Caux**. At the head of the valley, the market town of **Yvetot** is remarkable for its completely circular modern church, with windows by Max Ingrand that fairly take the breath away.

One can wander agreeably back towards the coast at Fécamp from here by zigzagging along minor roads and taking in the Château of Bailleul, its Renaissance facade framed by a lovely park, and then Valmont, whose ruined abbey church contains a fine, though roofless, Renaissance choir and an almost intact Lady Chapel of great beauty. **Fécamp** itself, wedged between steep cliffs, has a noble history dating back to the 1st century when, according to legend, a hollowed-out tree trunk bearing a box that contained some drops of Christ's blood beached at the head of its narrow harbour. It immediately became a place of pilgrimage: a monastery was founded in 606 which was replaced, after the Norsemen had flattened it, with a 10th-century Benedictine abbey. The Dukes of Normandy journeyed there at Easter time and it rivalled Mont-St. Michel in importance. After the abbey church had been struck by lightning (some of the Norman ruins remain) a Gothic one was built to replace it and called the Eglise de la Trinité. It is enormous, and much altered during subsequent centuries, and I find it gloomy, though it still attracts great crowds who also troop round the huge Benedictine distillery and museum (the liqueur was first concocted here in 1510), and stare curiously at the architecturally undistinguished fountain which marks the spot at which the Precious Blood came ashore. Today Fécamp's religious significance is somewhat obscured by its importance as a cod fishing port and the growth of allied industries such as curing and canning, and it has also managed to turn part of its seafront into a resort area. In contrast to Dieppe, however, its varied activities do not seem to cohabit happily.

Further west, Yport is a minute and picturesque spot in another dip in the cliffs but bigger **Etretat** is deservedly the queen of this part of the coast. Cliffs are again the inevitable frame, but they are wider spaced, reducing the feeling of claustrophobia, and eroded into weird and wonderful shapes. The British, who used to flock here to play golf on a splendid cliff-top course, and exchange enthusiastic platitudes in the *Golf Hotel Dormy House* bar, have now largely deserted it, but it remains busy and popular in the high season and, having kept a good deal of its cachet, is seldom totally deserted even in spring and autumn. A rebuilt covered market is the show-piece of the main square and there's a newish, cheerful hotel, the *Falaises*, between it and the seafront casino.

Inland from Etretat in the direction of Le Havre is some pretty country and one or two interesting spots: the diminutive churchyard at Cuverville is where André Gide is buried, and along a succession of tiny roads to the south of it lies the hamlet of Mannéglise, with a perfect gem of a small Romanesque church. Coming back towards Etretat up the Lézarde valley is the Château of Le Bec and, just beyond it, another Romanesque church at Turretot. It is hard to realise how near one is to the huge urbanised port complex of Le Havre when exploring these little corners, for it lies hidden below the level of the Caux plateau and, for all one sees of it, could easily belong to a different world.

Seine
Risle
Eure

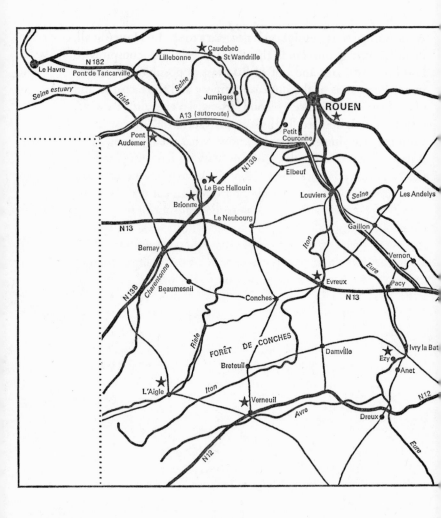

some leaning out over the streams (into which their sewage used to debouch), others meeting one another in vaulted archways across narrow blind alleys, yet others looking inwards on to tiny courtyards. In just such a house, James II of England spent a night in 1690, fleeing to Paris after his defeat at the Boyne.

St. Ouen's Church, in the rue de la République, spans several centuries and architectural styles and has some especially good Renaissance and modern stained glass; it was never given a final facade and, sitting at the café opposite it, I find myself speculating which of the many pockmarks on its rough stone exterior were put there as keys for the facade and which are the results of war. Also worth seeing is the *Auberge du Vieux Puits* restaurant, whose name is taken from the old well that was brought here in 1920 from the demolished Hotel du Cygne in Rouen, described by Flaubert in *Madame Bovary*. It is very good, but expensive; a smaller and quieter inn near the river is a more economical bet for an overnight stay.

For the right bank of the Seine, however, for Lillebonne, Caudebec and St. Wandrille, one should resist being siphoned onto the Tancarville Bridge and duck beneath it. Modern **Lillebonne** is nothing much, but it is one of the few places in Normandy with visible remains of the Roman occupation: the ruins of a 2nd-century theatre. And from it there is a view of the round tower of the castle keep where William the Conqueror assembled his nobles and persuaded them to take part in the invasion of 1066; although the tower was rebuilt a hundred and fifty years later, one is still spanning two momentous periods of history in a single glance.

Caudebec is a mere 16 kilometres (10 miles) from Lillebonne by the direct road. Sitting in a half-cylindrical scoop in the steep river bank, Caudebec was another Second World War casualty and is now fairly characterless except for its happy situation at the water's edge. But the 1940 conflagration that destroyed everything around it spared the glorious flamboyant Gothic church of Notre-Dame with its fantastic belfry and graceful interior. John Ruskin, that indefatigable chronicler both in words and drawings of fine architecture, sketched some of its intricate detail during his Normandy honeymoon in 1848, and used his last six minutes in town, before the stage-coach bore him away, to 'run back to the church and count some arches which I had missed'.

Sybarites as well as art-lovers come to Caudebec because it rejoices in one really excellent restaurant, the *Hôtel de la Marine* on the quayside, and one elegant hotel, the *Manoir de Rétival* on the cliff top to the east. There is a good but more modest hotel on the quayside, too. It also has a splendid, centuries-old Saturday market; while Ruskin was sketching the church his young wife, Effie, and their manservant George, were rhapsodising about the 'quantities of everything' they saw there, the flavour of the grapes they bought for a few *sous*, and the prodigious size of the pumpkins, which Effie measured and proclaimed to be 'seven feet round and six broad' (about 2.15 metres by 1.85 metres) which is 'pretty large for a fruit'.

I have never been able to get very enthusiastic about St. Wandrille, just east of Caudebec. It sits in a wooded hollow, partly obscured by the overhanging trees, and is built in an unexciting mixture of styles—some contributed in the 19th century by an English peer, Lord Stacpoole, who did a good deal of restoration while he was its tempoary owner. (Later, the writer Maurice Maeterlinck lived there for nine years; the monks returned in 1931.) I cannot speak for the much praised cloisters, since women are barred from them, but I find its history interesting. Founded in the 7th century (as Fontenelle) by a clever and reputedly personable young nobleman, it flourished as a seat of learning for two hundred years until destroyed by the Norse invaders, and was rebuilt (and renamed

Wandrille, after its founder) in the 10th century. The Benedictine monks were expelled during the French Revolution.

There are '*bacs*', or little ferries, that criss-cross the Seine at various points between the Tancarville Bridge and Rouen, and it can be entertaining to use these in fine weather instead of sticking to the main roads. Thus one can cross from Caudebec (the fees, incidentally, are the same as for the toll bridge) into the cool and peaceful Brotonne forest, and then take another *bac* across to the other side again for Jumièges.

Although a ruin, **Jumièges** has all the dramatic visual qualities that for me St. Wandrille lacks. Both were founded at about the same time and Jumièges was also razed during the Norman invasions and rebuilt afterwards. (Its abbey church, incidentally, was completed and consecrated in the year following the invasion of England; William the Conqueror, who was at the ceremony, presented it with Hayling Island, just off the Hampshire coast.) After the Revolution, it was used first as a builder's warehouse and later vandalised; it is now an ancient monument administered by the State.

A winter sun was slowly waning the first time I visited Jumièges and the guardian was about to lock up, but obligingly changed his mind when he learned that we were English. In that pale light the two magnificent towers of the west front, and the soaring roofless nave, made an impression that has never been bettered on subsequent visits, though the entire complex, which includes the smaller St. Pierre church, the chapter house, cloisters and store-rooms, repays hours of wandering.

Jumièges to Rouen is a quick hop by the main road, broken by a halt in the otherwise dull little suburb of St. Martin-de-Boscherville to see the church of St. Georges, now forlornly marooned in suburbia, that was once the centre of a huge 11th-century abbey. Or one can dawdle on the *bacs* again and come into Rouen from the south, crossing to Yville (sweet little château), taking a quick look at La Bouille, a pretty spot full of restaurants patronised by Rouennais on family outings, and at the Château of Robert the Devil nearby. (In fact, this fortress was probably built before the time of William the Conqueror's father, sometimes called 'le Diable'.) It was deliberately blown up to stop it falling into English hands during the Hundred Years War and its romantic ruins have not been improved by turning them into a sort of pleasure-garden, popular outing though they make for Rouen families.

Rouen itself demands a great deal of time if one is to know it well, and is impossible to encapsulate into a few pages, even though the wholesale destruction of the Second World War razed most of what the 1836 *Murray's Handbook for Travellers to France* described as its 'almost inextricable labyrinth of streets', which contained 'enough of antiquity to satiate . . . the most ardent lover of bygone times'. Now the historic part of the city that Ruskin so adored (putting it first of the 'three centres of my life's thought,') has shrunk to a relatively small area north of the Seine. So much even of this has had to be restored, too, that Ruskin would probably have had a stroke at the sight, for restoration was to him the most abysmal of crimes; one wonders how he would have advised the Rouennais to heal their shattered city if he had seen it in 1945. Possibly he would have wished them to prop up the more precious remains with plain concrete or stone, keeping only what was genuine for future ages. Not having seen Rouen in 1945, I have no way of knowing how bizarre that might have looked.

What the people of Rouen did do was to shift away from the centre the industries that had been increasingly clogging it since the 19th century; push a wide highway along the right bank of the river; create orderly and rather dull residential quarters where once the left bank factories were—and to leave the problem of car parks until it was almost too late. It is still a grave mistake to arrive by car thinking to 'do' the city in a day. Although most of the visible remains of its history—as Roman Rotomagus, as Normandy's first archbishopric, as the capital city of its first Duke, Rollo, and as the place where France's patron saint, Joan of Arc, met her death—have gone (as have the 'dirt and the bad smells' about which *Murray's Handbook* warned), there is still a great deal to see and one is better missing it altogether than spending half the time getting lost in one-way streets while trying to park, and the other half recovering from these exertions.

Most guide-book tours would have one walk in a roughly anti-clockwise circle starting in the Place du Vieux Marché, where a slab marks the place where Joan of Arc was burned. It was while I was hesitating by that spot one day that a friendly student got into conversation with me and urged me to start with a visit to the church of St. Gervais, a good kilometre away, because 'your king' died there. It took me a few seconds to realise he was speaking of William the Conqueror; he was the first and only Norman I have met who referred to 'votre roi' rather than 'notre duc Guillaume, le Conquérant'. So he guided me in a roundabout way to St. Gervais, via Pierre Corneille's much restored birthplace, and the hospital where Flaubert's doctor-father worked, and I was glad to have seen the dim 4th-century crypt which was William's first resting place. (Abandoned by his sons and courtiers as soon as he expired, he was only much later taken to the Abbaye aux Hommes in Caen for reburial—by all accounts a very pungent business.) Before steering me back to the Place du Vieux Marché he reminded me that in the cathedral crypt was another English tomb, that of Richard Coeur-de-Lion's brother, Henry; Richard's own heart was also originally buried there. Also in this crypt is the tomb of Louis de Brézé, husband of the formidable Diane de Poitiers; she is shown weeping beside him. She became the mistress of the Dauphin of France very early on in her widowhood, however, and held him, too. In 1547 the Dauphin became King Henri II and Diane the most powerful woman in France, a position she handled with apparent wisdom and dignity until the King himself was killed in a tournament in 1559. Diane survived him by nearly twenty years and died at Anet, the castle she built further south, at the very respectable age of sixty-nine.

But one does not start a tour of Rouen with the cathedral crypt; one comes to this gradually, from the Place du Vieux Marché, circuiting to look at the sumptuous courtyard of the former Bourgtheroulde mansion (it rhymes with 'Gertrude', and is now the offices of a bank) and sauntering slowly along the rue du Gros Horloge. Here is the 14th-century belfry and, looking slightly incongruous beside it, the Great Clock (Gros Horloge) itself, which was removed from the belfry in the 16th century and placed upon a low archway that acquired its present florid appearance in 1892.

Now one begins to see the west front of the cathedral, with its two totally different towers, the St. Romain one on a Romanesque base and the Beurre one in pure flamboyant Gothic. Once one gets used to the fact that Rouen Cathedral underwent its first 'restoration' in 1200, and that almost every later age has contributed to it in different architectural styles, it becomes increasingly compulsive; after a while one ceases to have reservations over what may or may not be original and simply abandons oneself to the enjoyment of a rich architectural confection. The same goes for the rest of Old Rouen; the Bureau des Finances building, facing the Beurre tower and housing the Tourist Office, was built in 1510 in early Renaissance style; behind the cathedral (where there are some well-restored timber-framed houses in the rue St. Romain) the St. Maclou church, though finished slightly later than the Bureau des Finances, is pure flamboyant Gothic and perhaps the most harmonious building in the city. (Its cloisters, separate from it, served as a cemetery in the Middle Ages, for plague victims among others.) Up rue Damiette, with its cafés and antique shops, St. Ouen dates from the early 14th century but was given a new facade in the mid-19th; it was once an abbey church and the much restored Town Hall, beside it, was originally part of the complex. Beyond it is the Lycée Corneille where not only Pierre Corneille was educated but also Flaubert, Maupassant and André Maurois. Another famous pupil was Robert de la Salle, the 17th-century explorer who crossed from French Canada to lay claim to Ohio and subsequently navigated the Ohio and Mississippi rivers south to the Gulf of Mexico. Beyond the Lycée is the Musée d'Antiquités which contains a particularly good collection of Roman finds from Lillebonne, and another museum that should not be missed is the Beaux-Arts, with a fascinating Rouen Ceramics section. From here one can either saunter north to the so-called Tour Jeanne d'Arc, the keep and only remaining portion of Philippe-Auguste's castle, built after he captured Rouen in 1204, and where St. Joan was imprisoned by the English in 1430, or come back to the Place du Vieux Marché via the lovingly restored wedding-cake facade of the Palais de Justice in the rue aux Juifs. Return to the Place du Vieux Marché one must, though, to have a meal at *La Couronne*, possibly the oldest restaurant in France (founded in 1345) where the *Caneton à la Rouennaise* is quite unbelievably delicious.

Before moving on, there are two little pilgrimages that lovers of French literature can make: to the Flaubert Pavilion at **Croisset**, and to Corneille's house at **Petit-Couronne**. The Flaubert museum, still very much in the Rouen suburbs, was once a pavilion in the grounds of the writer's house, since demolished, and contains some rather touching souvenirs. Continuing south along the edge of the Roumare forest, a *bac* lower down disembarks one near Petit-Couronne and the former country house of Pierre Corneille's father, pleasantly

45

arranged and reverently cared for.

After a brief halt here, I find little to detain me on this bank of the Seine; the strange rocks and cliff caves of Orival appeal to walkers, as does the view of the Seine from the top, but Elbeuf is purely industrial. I am inclined to get on to the *autoroute* at Grande Couronne and stay on it until the Louviers-Evreux exit, even though it means missing the agreeable little town of Pont-de-l'Arche, where the first bridge over the lower Seine was built.

Louviers, on the other hand, is well worth a stop. Although on the Eure and not the Seine it does, thanks to the Seine's meanderings, lie almost halfway along the direct route from Rouen to Vernon. Quieter since the *autoroute* was built, it has been a wool town since the 13th century and its Notre-Dame church was built as much in testimony to the wealth of its merchants as to the glory of God. The south side is particularly overwhelming in the lacy intricacy of its detail. Louviers has some nice old houses, and a collection of Rouen ceramics in its little museum, and just outside the town is the wildly eccentric 16th-17th-century manor house of St. Hilaire, a bizarre assembly of half-timbering, towers, turrets and abruptly angled roofs.

Coming back towards the Seine and Vernon again, **Gaillon** is the next obvious milestone, and an interesting one because its enormous ruined castle, built at the turn of the 15th and 16th centuries, was the first Renaissance château in Normandy. But it is hard to resist the temptation to detour right into the loop of the Seine first, even if one does not actually cross it, for a glimpse of Château Gaillard at **Les Andelys** on the opposite bank.

Richard Coeur-de-Lion's precipitously perched fortress was built with astonishing speed—though probably not within the single year claimed in some accounts—when in 1196 he decided a greater deterrent was needed to keep the King of France away from Rouen. It was only to survive intact for some seven years, however, for after Richard's death Philippe-Auguste of France stormed it in 1204. It did not immediately fall into disrepair: it was made use of in 1314 as a prison for two sad princesses, Blanche and Marguerite, the wives of Charles IV and Louis X respectively; Marguerite was strangled there. Its partial demolition took place in 1603, by permission of Henri IV. The view from the top is quite stupendous, and there are a few modest hotels in the village below it, the nicest being the *Chaine d'Or*.

Continuing to Vernon, the right bank of the Seine is prettier than the other side (which is a good reason for crossing the river rather than simply gazing at Château Gaillard from afar). At **Vernon**, before re-crossing the Seine, one wants to take a little side street to where the crumbling towers of the Château des Tourelles stand in an oasis of greenery near the river bank; it used to guard the approach to the 12th-century bridge. There is a nice view of these ancient supports, and of a scatter of islands, from the new bridge which leads to the town centre. Here is the much altered church of Notre-Dame; some charming old wood-frame houses in the streets around it, and the extravagantly over-restored Tour des Archives, once a castle keep.

Before leaving Vernon, art-lovers might make a little side trip further upstream on the right bank to the village of Giverny, where Claude Monet lived for over forty years, gradually turning it into an artists' colony.

Here this survey leaves the Seine and moves southwards and westwards, back to the Eure and the lovely rural stock-farming landscapes of the Pays d'Ouche. Pacy-sur-Eure is only 13 kilometres (about 8 miles) from Vernon; it has some interesting modern art, particularly glass, in its St. Aubin church.

47

The Eure south of Pacy winds through country that is edged with gentle hills and the occasional low escarpment. **Ivry-la-Bataille** has a 16th-century church with a much older south doorway; the *bataille* after which it is named was Henri IV's victory in 1590 over the Catholic Leaguers, just six months after he had resisted their siege at Arques, near Dieppe. Far more fascinating are the remains of Diane de Poitiers' castle at **Anet**, just south of it (with the excellent *Auberge Maître Corbeau* conveniently placed on the opposite bank at **Ezy**). Most people associate Chenonceaux, in the Loire valley, with Diane, and of course that castle was hers too. But after twenty-six years of unparalleled influence over Henri II, his mistress when he was Dauphin as well as King, she lost Chenonceaux to Henri II's wife, Catherine de Medici, on the King's death in 1559 and retired to Anet which he had started to have built for her just after his accession in 1547. As one might expect of this elegant and composed lady, who took regular cold baths and dressed almost exclusively in black and white (perhaps in mourning for her husband; perhaps simply because they suited her), she employed the best architect (Philibert Delorme) and artists of the day to make Anet a monument to impeccable good taste in the Italian Renaissance style; the original bas-relief above the gateway arch was by Benvenuto Cellini (it is now in the Louvre, having been replaced by a copy). Those parts of the castle that have survived the ravages of time and the Revolution are extraordinarily evocative and contain numerous relics of Diane de Poitiers, including her bed with its original hangings. Her splendid black and white marble tomb is in the pretty, barrel-vaulted pinkish brick chapel adjoining the castle.

The road from Anet to Dreux continues to follow the Eure, passing the ruins of the former Abbey of Breuil-Benoit whose church dates from the 12th century. **Dreux** itself, once a frontier-town fortified by the Kings of France against the

Dukes of Normandy, and now a market town, is not on the Eure but on its tributary, the Blaise, and is chiefly known for its Chapelle Royale St. Louis, the mausoleum of the Orléans family. Louis-Philippe, great-great-grandson of Louis XIV, who came to the French throne in 1830, was an Orléans on his father's side; his mother was of the ruling family of Dreux and built a chapel there in 1816. Louis-Philippe enlarged and vastly embellished it and the result is a fanciful 19th-century monument in a park-like setting. Down near the river, in the town centre, is a strange free-standing belfry, part flamboyant Gothic and part Renaissance; across the main square from it is the much restored church of St. Pierre.

Dreux is almost outside the boundaries of Normandy; coming back northwards towards Evreux one passes through Nonancourt, one of the original fortress-towns that guarded the Duchy's southern boundary along the Avre. Two more, to the west of it, were Tillières and **Verneuil**, the latter by far the most interesting of the three, with vestiges of the old fortifications, some splendid old houses dating back to the 15th century, and a handful of pleasant hotels and restaurants. The little *Hôtel du Saumon* and the *Grand Sultan* restaurant are both close to its best-known church, La Madeleine. Rather heavily restored, it is not, to my mind, as harmonious as the Romanesque Notre-Dame which has some particularly good 16th-century statuary.

But all the churches of this part of Normandy defer to **Evreux's** Notre-Dame Cathedral, at the heart of the little city that lies on the twisting Iton, midway between the Risle and the Seine and some 28 kilometres (18 miles) inside Normandy's southern border. Its history is almost a microcosm of Norman history: first Roman, then occupied and fortified by the Goths; then sacked by Vandals and Normans, then burned in 1119 by the English and in 1193 by the French, under Philippe-Auguste; burned yet again in 1356 and battered in 1379; face-lifted not entirely successfully by that 19th-century arch-restorer, Viollet-le-Duc; burned and damaged yet again during the Second World War.

Each disaster, however, only spurred its people to new efforts: Evreux and its cathedral have been built and rebuilt with a patience and courage that is quite phenomenal. Today a neat little market town with a few industries on the outskirts, its new buildings are nicely planned to show off the old ones. The cathedral, incorporating details from almost every stage of its existence, is extraordinarily absorbing. Perhaps its most remarkable feature, even so close to Chartres, is the stained glass that Proust made a special journey to see. One could happily linger a day or two here staying at *Le Grand Cerf* which overlooks the west front and where one feeds magnificently. There are other sights to be seen, too, including the equally patched-up St. Taurin church; the 15th-century clock tower, and the former Bishop's Palace. Evreux also has a couple of reasonable bed-and-breakfast hotels, the *Grenoble* and the *de l'Orme*; it thus makes a good centre for exploring the entire region south of Rouen between the Seine and the Risle.

To the west (a minor road from Evreux that follows the Iton, and then crosses the main road to follow the little valley of the Rouloir, is extremely pretty) is **Conches-en-Ouche** with its huge forest beyond it, and here is yet another church, Ste. Foy, containing some memorable stained glass. Conches in fact is a pleasant little town altogether, spared by the war and typically Norman, with a ruined castle on its heights and a terrace between it and Ste. Foy, from which there are lovely views over the Rouloir valley.

North of Conches, and north-west of Evreux, is the great plain of Neubourg, with **Le Neubourg** at its heart. Tourists do not come here very much, and yet it has a strange charm compounded of immense spaces that almost melt into the sky. Here and there a line of trees marches across the emptiness like a ghostly column of soldiers; elsewhere are clumps of yews and the spires of country churches, sometimes angular and slate-faced, sometimes all stone with saddleback roofs. There are some splendid châteaux, too, Omonville at **Le Tremblay-Omonville,** just south of Le Neubourg, and the two great Harcourt domains to the west of it. One of the oldest and most aristocratic families in all France, let alone Normandy, the Harcourts regained possession of Champ-de-Bataille after the Second World War, in part restitution for the destruction of Thury-Harcourt in 1944. A magnificent 17th-century building, consisting of two wings linked by porticos enclosing a vast courtyard, it is full of wonderful furniture, paintings and *objets d'art*. Nearby, the other Harcourt château, called by the family name, is administered by the State and, although the buildings are not open to the public, the grounds are. They are unique, too, being planted with rare and splendid trees, and as one wanders about the park one can see the massive fortified castle gateway with its two square flanking towers.

Harcourt is on the very edge of the Neubourg plain, where it starts to drop away to the Risle valley; and Brionne, sitting astride this pretty little river, makes a pleasant centre for exploring in both directions.

To the south is the strange little 11th-century chapel of St. Eloi with a spring welling up from beneath it that was almost certainly the centre of a much earlier Gallo-Roman cult. Even today pilgrimages are made to the chapel. Not far from St. Eloi is the confluence of the Risle and the Charentonne, which between them form an almost perfect oval since the Charentonne rises close to the infant Risle about 50 kilometres (30 miles) further inland. Thus one can make a pleasant circular tour from Brionne, down the Risle valley with its pretty churches at Beaumontel, Beaumont-le-Roger and La Ferrière, skirting the western edge of the Forest of Conches and coming finally to **l'Aigle,** an unassuming but agreeable little town where they make pins and needles and which, unexpectedly, has an extremely good hotel-restaurant, the *Dauphin*. At some point, perhaps from Beaumont, one wants to make a detour to **Beaumesnil** for a look at the immensely formal 17th-century facade of the moated château there, its central portion tall, steep-roofed and stiffly ornate and its two flanking pavilions low and almost apologetic in contrast, rather like an aristocratic aunt sitting upright in an armchair.

Then from l'Aigle one can cut across to **St. Evroult-Notre-Dame-du-Bois**, where are the lovely, evocative remains of a once great abbey, and return by the pretty Charentonne valley. There is a beautiful rural view, spiked by two village church steeples, from the war memorial just before Montreuil-d'Argillé, and next comes Broglie, a little market town that became the seat of a princely family of Italian origin.

Bernay, where the Cosnier runs into the Charentonne, is an attractive little town; there is a splendid general view of it from the Promenade des Monts on the edge of the hill above. It repays a longer pause, too, for the Town Hall building was once the ancient abbey, founded early in the 11th century, and beside it is the former abbey church. After Bernay come the enchanting villages of Menneval and Fontaine-l'Abbé, with its castle; then Serquigny, still possessing a church with an unusual black and white west front, and then one is back on the road to **Brionne**.

I am fond of this modest little town of islets formed by branches of the Risle, watched over by an imposing square Norman castle-keep on a hilltop to the east. With two nice small hotels (the *Logis de Brionne* is the one I have patronised most often) it is an alternative stopping place to its more famous neighbour, **Le Bec-Hellouin**—though the two are inextricably linked, and it would be unthinkable not to sample some truly Norman cuisine at the *Auberge de l'Abbaye* at Le Bec.

The great abbey which is the core, heart and soul of Le Bec-Hellouin (the village, indeed, is more like a cathedral close) was founded in 1034 by a Norman knight. For nearly a decade it was a small and wretchedly poor community until it was joined by a learned Italian called Lanfranc; thenceforth, thanks to his reputation as a teacher, the monastery prospered and flourished: St. Evroult-Notre-Dame-du-Bois was its dependency.

From Le Bec stemmed the entire religious organisation of mediaeval England, for in the process of subduing the nobles of his Duchy young Duke William besieged Brionne in 1050, and met Lanfranc between bouts of belligerence. As a result, Lanfranc became William's most trusted counsellor; he induced the Pope to lift the interdict placed on Normandy after William's marriage to his cousin Matilda; he subsequently became Abbot of William's Abbaye aux Hommes at Caen and, eventually, Archbishop of Canterbury—in which role he virtually ruled England when William was absent. Other illustrious products of Le Bec were Lanfranc's successor there, Anselm, who also succeeded him at Canterbury, and Gundulf, Lanfranc's secretary, who later became Bishop of Rochester and the original architect of the Tower of London.

The abbey buildings are much restored, for the monks were expelled during the French Revolution and the church later demolished. It was brought back to life and restored after the Second World War but the church was never rebuilt; its ruins are among the most impressive parts of the present complex.

Two more rewarding little tours can be made in the other direction from Brionne. One is up the valley of the Livet to the Château of Launay. Visitors cannot enter the castle but there is a lovely view of it from the main gate, along a broad drive flanked with beautiful half-timbered outbuildings and a pair of enchanting dovecotes. The other, in exactly the opposite direction, is to the Château of Tilly near **Boissey-le-Châtel**, in the direction of Bourgtheroulde. It was built in 1500 by a

Lord of Bourgtheroulde whose town house in Rouen now houses a bank.

One can come back to the Risle through the Forest of Montfort, via the pretty village of Ecaquelon, and from Montfort-sur-Risle there is a nice shady road that follows the river down to Pont Audemer.

Côte Fleurie
Pays d'Auge

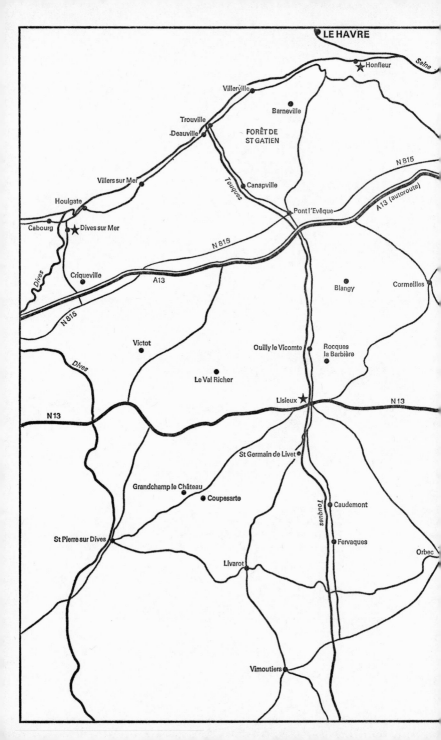

I have another favourite breakfast stop after an early morning disembarkation at Le Havre: **Honfleur**. (Being an indifferent sailor, I prefer the Channel by night, and the breakfast venue depends on my eventual direction.) Honfleur of course deserves a far longer stay than the mere consumption of coffee and croissants requires, but I like it best in the early morning nonetheless. The road along the south side of the Seine estuary rises and dips between hedges and apple orchards drenched in dew; the gateways to some of the churches and bigger houses have little thatched roofs from whose ridges irises grow—a decorative way of keeping the rain out. Inland of this stretch of road the boy later to become William the Conqueror lived with his mother and her husband, Herlwin de Conteville, safe from the warring Norman nobles until he was old enough to command them; it would be enthralling to know exactly where in the tiny village of Conteville the house stood.

Arriving at Honfleur, I make for one of the cafés overlooking the inner port, or Vieux Bassin; few tourists are about and the customers are mostly fishermen and other workers in *bleu de travail*, tossing down one *p'tit Calva* (tiny glassful of Calvados) after another between cups of coffee, and rumbling on in deep, heavily accented voices.

From the café, or the cobbles in front of it if it is warm enough, one can savour the vista of multi-coloured boats surrounded by the tall, narrow, slate-roofed houses made familiar by so many famous painters. The present Vieux Bassin was built in the 17th century, in the reign of Louis XIV, replacing an earlier one that had become silted up; the Lieutenance buildings at the seaward end are all that remain of the earlier fortifications. It has always been a starting point for explorers and navigators: Samuel Champlain, who colonised

Quebec, sailed from Honfleur in the 17th century, and several thousand Norman peasants gradually followed him to settle there.

In the course of time this port, too, became silted up, and then the artists took over, starting in the early 19th century when the fashionable court painter, Isabey, discovered this coast. He was followed by Richard Bonnington, the English water-colourist, and Jongkind, a Dutchman, but it was the son of an Honfleur paddle-steamer captain, Eugène Boudin, who established his native port as the artistic capital of the early Impressionists. At the *Ferme St. Siméon*, then a simple inn and now justly renowned, they would meet and drink cider and talk of life and of painting: Corot, Monet, Sisley, Pissarro, Cézanne and others.

Many of Boudin's paintings, and those of other Honfleur artists, are to be seen in the Boudin museum, and their devotees still crouch behind easels all over Honfleur—not merely round the Vieux Bassin but in the Place Ste. Catherine, with its ancient wooden church and queerly shaped free-standing belfry, around which the market is held, and on almost every street corner of this entrancing little town.

From Honfleur the main road more or less follows the coast westwards, through farmlands and orchard country with the feathery St. Gatien forest just inland; somewhere here William the Conqueror's mother and her husband are buried— at Grestain, they say, but I have never managed to find it. There is a pretty little creeper-covered 12th-century church at Cricqueboeuf, and then the little resort of Villerville. **Trouville**, a few miles further, lies on the right bank of the Touques and in fact grew up from the original port of Touques, where Henry V landed in 1417, two years after Agincourt. The quayside is still very much the heart of Trouville, with its lively fish market and bus station; even out of season, when the imposing Casino is deserted, Trouville still feels alive. Its long beach and the little streets of houses and small hotels behind it were fashionable long before Deauville, west of the Touques, was ever thought of; Dumas père was one of its earliest regular visitors and by the mid-19th century Flaubert was complaining that it was already too popular. Whistler stayed there in 1865; in 1870 the Empress Eugénie escaped from here in an English yacht; later still, Marcel Proust frequented the now vanished Hôtel des Roches Noires, and although today's *beau monde* patronises much newer Deauville, its twin resort still has a faithful following.

Deauville is—Deauville: well laid out, meticulously groomed, managing to keep up to date with new apartment complexes and marinas that cunningly blend with its Second Empire and turn-of-the-century architectural follies. It is particularly amusing in the peak summer season when all the branches of the smart Paris shops are open, and the races are on, and balls and galas succeed one another almost nightly. Between spells of strolling along the Promenade des Planches, the board-walk that edges the fine sand beach, and observing the beautiful people, or riding or sailing or playing tennis or swimming or patronising the Casino, there are gentle little excursions to be made. Just inland, beyond the old village of Touques, is **Canapville**, with the ancient wooded manor of the Bishops of Lisieux, and **Bonneville**, still harbouring a few remains of the castle where William the Conqueror organised the invasion of England. To the east is the less historic but more obviously photogenic **St. Andre d'Hébertot**, a charming ensemble of hamlet, lake, park and moated château; and the fine manor house of Barneville.

Deauville's cachet fades visibly as one moves westwards through its outskirts, but **Villers-sur-Mer** is worth a stop when the weather favours a brisk walk along the beach, for it is at the centre of a vast sweep of sand that in part runs beneath the chalk cliffs known as the Vaches Noires, a local beauty spot. Beyond them is **Houlgate**, a quiet, typically Norman resort that has not yet been overwhelmed by the strident seventies and beyond again is the mouth of the river Dives.

The road swings inland a bit here, and bypasses the remains of the one-time port of **Dives-sur-Mer**. Thanks to a shifting of the coastline, Dives is no longer 'sur mer', but in 1066 it was the assembly point for the Norman invasion fleet. A 19th-century engraved list of some of the invaders' names can be seen in Dives' surprisingly large 14th–15th-century Notre-Dame church. Also worth looking at are the timbered market halls, of slightly later date, but the famous old coaching inn, the *Hostellerie Guillaume le Conquérant*, is now largely rebuilt to house flats and craft boutiques and a restaurant named after its distinguished antecedent.

Across the river from Dives is the last of the Côte Fleurie resorts, **Cabourg**, forever associated with Proust. Together with Trouville, it was the principal Norman ingredient of his imaginary 'Balbec'; indeed, he wrote most of his *A la Recherche du Temps Perdu* (*Remembrance of Things Past*) here, and also used it as a source of material for *A l'Ombre des Jeunes Filles en Fleurs* (*Within a Budding Grove*). It still has an other-worldly feel; even its layout is quaint, with streets radiating like a sunburst away from the seafront *Grand Hôtel* and Casino. The primly ornate little houses and hotels, discreetly fronted by rows of pollarded limes, have a toy-like look; out of season, the impression is of an elaborate nursery construction that has been abandoned for some more positive pleasure. Each time I approach it, I am half afraid that some bulldozing nursery-maid will have tidied it all away. But the sight of the Crèmerie d'Isigny in the Avenue de la Mer, with its earthenware bowls of thick cream and huge bricks of pale butter, is an enduring reassurance that Cabourg has not been face-lifted.

Inland of the Côte Fleurie, the Pays d'Auge represents for most people the quintessence of rural Normandy: green, wooded, and gently rolling, where speckled cows graze among the apple orchards (bright with blossom from about mid-April and with little red cider apples in the autumn) and timber-framed farms and manors keep their ancient places. The ravages of time and warfare have taken their toll of many of those traditional buildings, though; I have never managed a satisfactory photograph combining the three main elements of cows, apple-blossom and timber-framed barn.

But gastronomical compensations abound: Pays d'Auge cider, Calvados and good cooking, all to be found in scores of excellent country and village restaurants. The cider, only very faintly fizzy, can be pale-gold or pinkish, full-bodied or dry, and is made from apples that were originally introduced from Navarre, in the Basque country. It is normally drunk young; once, in February, I had to 'make do' with wine in a restaurant reputed for its own cider, because the new vintage was not quite à point and last year's had run out. Calvados, the spirit distilled from apple juice, needs on the other hand to be at least twelve years old before the faint-hearted can appreciate it, and even then it is searingly powerful. But it perfectly complements rich Norman cooking: the *trou normand*, consisting of a little glass of Calvados halfway through a meal, may make the uninitiated feel slightly dizzy but does wonders for the digestion.

As for the cheeses, the soft and creamy Pont l' Evêque is the oldest-established and most typical of the Pays d'Auge, but the strong-smelling Livarot dates back nearly as far—some six hundred years. Effie Ruskin, on her protracted Normandy honeymoon with John, did not appreciate it: 'How the people eat it is a marvel to me for it is . . . kept until it is in the last stage of decay with the most disgusting smell possible.' (Perhaps if she had tried it in the restaurant of Livarot's *Hôtel du Vivier*, she might have appreciated it better.) Camembert, best-known and most copied of all French cheeses, comes from further south and is comparatively new on the cheese scene: less than two hundred years old. But the varieties made elsewhere are surprisingly different from the real stuff; one has only to bring along a sample of what one normally buys at home to verify this.

Whether one comes to the Pays d'Auge from the south and east, by way of Paris and Evreux, or from the north, via Le Havre and Pont l'Evêque (whose position on a busy cross-roads has rather dimmed its attractions, except as a producer of cheese and Calvados), **Lisieux** is the natural centre. Thanks to its importance as a place of pilgrimage (it was the birthplace of St. Teresa of Lisieux, to whose cult a vast basilica has been built) the town has a great many smallish hotels and (provided one chooses a place with its own parking, like the *Lisieux*) could be a convenient touring base. The basilica, and most of the other pilgrimage shrines, are in a newish quarter to the south of the town proper. But the rest of the town is mostly modern too, for almost all of its original buildings, including whole streets of houses dating back to the 13th century, were burned during the 1944 bombardments.

By some miracle, the Cathedral of St. Pierre was spared and although rather girt about by post-war rebuilding, is still a fine sight. Begun in about 1170 at the instigation of Bishop Arnoul, who had officiated at the marriage of Henry II of England and Eleanor of Aquitaine in a church on the same spot some twenty years earlier, it was finished in under a hundred years. Its west front, facing a busy square, has a trio of doorways framed between two dissimilar towers rising above a flight of steps, but one enters by the south transept doorway, called the Gateway to Paradise, coming to the heart of the beautifully proportioned interior beneath the magnificent lantern tower.

Multitudes of entrancing spots surround Lisieux: to the north, Ouilly-le-Vicomte, with one of Normandy's oldest churches (heavily restored after war damage in 1944); neighbouring Rocques, whose 13th-century church has twin wooden porches, and beyond them the pretty old towns of Blangy-le-Château and Cormeilles. To the north-west is Val-Richer, a former abbey converted in the 19th century into the home of a local Parliamentary deputy, and redolent of his wealth and worthiness. Beyond that, by a series of pretty byways, is the 16th-century Pré d'Auge ceramic-tiled manor house of Victot, in a lovely setting, and beyond that again, on the other side of the *autoroute*, the mediaeval brick and stone chequered Château of Cricqueville-en-Auge.

The most remarkably patterned of all the Pays d'Auge manor houses, however, is due south of Lisieux: moated St. Germain-de-Livet, which belongs to the city and can be visited. Its exterior is a mosaic of glazed blues, greens and pinks, and some of its upstairs rooms are also tiled. The nearby Touques valley road passes yet more picturesque castles and manors: Caudemone, imposing Fervaques, Bellou (a small detour) and Chiffretôt. Just south of this is **Vimoutiers**, an important butter and cheese township that has risen from the ashes of 1944. In the main square is one statue (presented by American cheesemakers) of Marie Harel, the farmer's wife who gave the world Camembert, and there is another in the town plus a memorial at the crossroads to the south, leading to the village that gave the cheese its name. Less well known is the fact that the young and beautiful Charlotte Corday also came from this area: she was born on a farm near the hamlet of Les Champeaux across the fields from Camembert. She it was who, filled with revolutionary ideals and disillusioned by the increasing autocracy of Marat, stabbed him to death in his bath in 1793.

One can circle back to Lisieux from Vimoutiers in two completely opposite directions, creating a painful choice. One way is via **Orbec**, a sweet old town in the wooded valley of the Orbiquet; it has one really superb restaurant (*Au Caneton*) where they do duckling quite miraculously, and the modest

Hôtel de France that would make a pleasantly rural touring base. The other circuit is alluring too: via Livarot to the little market town of **St. Pierre-sur-Dives**, whose wonderfully sturdy church has survived many a vicissitude and spans several centuries: the pillars of the triforium are of Roman origin and were part of the 12th-century church. The chapter house has a floor of extremely rare and lovely 13th-century ceramic tiles that are well worth taking some trouble to see (one must seek out the sacristan), and the covered market is a lovingly faithful restoration of the original mediaeval building, destroyed in 1944. And on the way back to Lisieux from St. Pierre are two more glorious manor houses, just off the main road to either side of it: Grandchamp to the west, and moated, timber-framed Coupesarte to the east.

Conqueror's Country

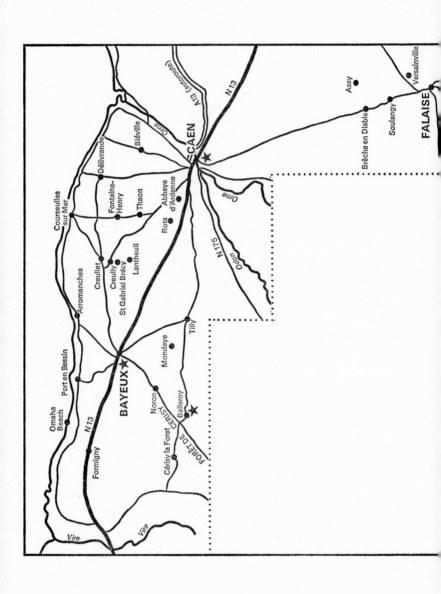

St. Pierre-sur-Dives is almost on the imaginary border that separates the lyrical Pays d'Auge from the region most closely associated with William the Conqueror. Its heart, of course, is Caen, reached from St. Pierre or Lisieux by a variety of ways—of which I prefer the one from **Falaise**, Duke William's birthplace, for although it lies well south of the direct route it seems to me the chronologically correct starting place.

The approach to Falaise from Lisieux and St. Pierre is not the most dramatic, but if one takes a little side road that passes the Château of Versainville instead of sticking to the main road, one can not only enjoy a graceful 18th-century facade but at least get some idea of the setting of Falaise as one comes down into it. The most spectacular view of the town, whose name means 'cliff', is however from the south and west, where one can best appreciate how the castle and ramparts literally rise from the summit of an abrupt escarpment of the Ante valley.

Despite the fact that Falaise was horribly damaged in August 1944, and is consequently largely rebuilt, and despite the fact that its castle is almost certainly not the one in which William was born, it still manages to evoke a strong sense of the links between Normandy and Britain. The great bronze equestrian statue of Duke William that dominates the main square, and the inscription on its plinth that proclaims him '*Guillaume le Conquérant, Duc de Normandie, Roi d'Angleterre*', gets the priorities firmly right.

The story of the beautiful tanner's daughter, Arlette (or Herlève), who caught the eye of William's father and, disdaining any secret assignations, rode proudly into the castle by the main gateway, is an appealing one. I know that the guide is indulging in poetic licence when he points out 'the self-same window' through which Duke Robert first spied Arlette, and to the 'self-same chamber' in which their son saw the light of day, but it does not detract from the romantic aura of the grassy, rock-strewn ruins: the keep dates from only a couple of hundred years after William's birth and probably stands on the same foundations, and I enjoy this harmless fiction. (So, apparently, did Ruskin and Effie, who spent a week at Falaise and revelled in the castle and its legends.)

Unfortunately, by the time the little charade is over, I am less disposed to appreciate the Gothic and Renaissance detail of the church of La Trinité, opposite the Duke's statue, though it has some lively carvings on the pillars in the nave. St. Gervais, of which one of Ruskin's drawings survives, is more unusual; half Romanesque and half Gothic, the two styles solemnly facing each other across the nave.

There are some pleasant halts to be made on the road from Falaise to Caen, having perhaps stayed overnight in Falaise, at either the *Normandie* or the *Poste* hotels. Aubigny has a fine castle on its outskirts and a little row of exceptionally interesting funerary statues in its church. Soulangy, with its majestic belfry, is another pause; so is the Brèche du Diable gorge, above which stands the florid tomb of the actress Marie Joly; and so is the theatrical facade of the neo-classical Château of Assy—these last two necessitating a slight detour.

Caen is another largely reconstructed city; more than half of it was burned and bombarded during the summer of 1944, including the famous old streets which the 19th-century *Murray's Handbook* described as wider than those of Rouen, and more cheerful, and which needed 'days to explore', and scores of magnificent and historic houses, including the one in which Charlotte Corday lived. But modern Caen has been thoughtfully planned and has one important feature in common with its predecessor: the pale Caen stone which imparts quality to even the least distinguished modern building. Now a thriving industrial centre and port, Caen was relatively insignificant until, about the middle of the 11th century, Duke William made it his capital. Having with some trouble won the hand of his cousin Matilda of Flanders, who was loth to wed a bastard (he persuaded her to change her mind in true caveman style, by dragging her about her chamber by the hair), he then found himself in more trouble with the Pope, who disapproved of the blood relationship. After Lanfranc had managed to get the Papal interdict rescinded, the couple demonstrated their repentance by building great abbeys at either end of the city: William's Abbaye aux Hommes and Matilda's Abbaye aux Dames, both of which have survived many vicissitudes, including a sacking by Edward III of England in 1346, and another by Henry V in 1417. Henry V repaired much of the damage his army had done to Caen and the English ruled it for thirty-three years; in 1432 Henry VI founded the university, the first in France.

The church of St. Etienne in the Abbaye aux Hommes is Caen's principal monument; although its choir, and the Gothic spires on the west front towers, date from the 13th century, and although it was restored in the 17th century, it remains in essence much as it was when William and Lanfranc first built it: noble and austere. Ruskin found it 'too cold to stay in' (although he and Effie spent a week in Caen, he disliked it and did no sketches of St. Etienne), but to the people of Caen it is not just the principal church but also a symbol, which should mean something to the English too: while it stands, the English throne will endure. Thus in the 1944 bombardment many hundreds of citizens took refuge in St. Etienne—and were spared for their faith. (It should be added that the more secular-minded who sheltered in the stone quarries outside town also survived.) William, England's first Norman king, was eventually buried in St. Etienne, having died in Rouen, but only a slab marks the spot, for the tomb was first plundered during the Religious Wars and again during the Revolution.

The former abbey buildings that flank St. Etienne now contain the Town Hall and municipal offices, and retain many handsome features.

Before crossing the town centre, it is worth going along the narrow streets to the north of St. Etienne to find the tiny and quite untouched 11th-century Romanesque church of St. Nicholas, deconsecrated now and surrounded by a shaggy, overgrown cemetery. Coming back eastward along the rue Ecuyère and the Place des Ecuyers, one joins the main shopping street of Caen, the rue St. Pierre, in which two ancient houses still remain. Near them is St. Sauveur, which Ruskin sketched from a café opposite. In one of his letters home, admirably edited by J. G. Links*, he explodes disgustedly about the un-Christian behaviour of the café's fellow patrons; indeed he had nothing good to say about Caen or its people. There is a pathetic story from an earlier age associated with St. Sauveur, though—or perhaps the association was with the Vieux St. Sauveur church, just behind this one—for it was the Bon Sauveur nuns who cared for Beau Brummell in his madness and old age. The famous dandy, having fallen from courtly grace in England, came here as British Consul in 1830, only to be made redundant two years later. Thereafter, mounting debts led to his being gaoled, a state from which French friends rescued him as his English ones had deserted him. He was already half mad, living at the Hôtel d'Angleterre and from time to time going through the motions of giving elegant parties to which no one came; the 19th-century writer Barbey d'Aurevilly left a touching description of one such charade. The Hôtel d'Angleterre no longer exists, of course, but there is a very agreeable one with an excellent restaurant (*Le Dauphin*) just north of rue St. Pierre and near the castle. And several good though more modest restaurants like the *Poêle d'Or* and the *Pomme d'Api* are to be found to the south, in the

* *The Ruskins in Normandy* (John Murray, 1968).

triangle made by the Bassin St. Pierre and the course of the Orne; these are the places in which to eat the famous *tripes à la mode de Caen.*

At the end of the rue St. Pierre is the richly ornamented Gothic church of the same name, standing opposite the remains of Caen Castle, splendidly isolated within a girdle of green lawns. Beyond it, up the rue des Chanoines, is Queen Matilda's Abbaye aux Dames and La Trinité church, now partly attatched to the hospital. It is less harmonious than St. Etienne, but the Queen's mausoleum is impressive.

Ruskin thought the country between Caen and Bayeux 'quite ugly', and certainly it does not compare with the Pays d'Auge. But it is far from ugly, despite the terrible battles fought over it, and there is plenty to see, so that one can easily take a whole day getting from one place to the other although they are only 27 kilometres (about 17 miles) apart. A little circuit of the Odon valley to the south-west will give the military-minded some idea of the awful fighting that took place here; there are monuments at strategic spots.

To the west and north are more peaceful sights: the ruins of the 12th-century Abbey of Ardenne; the churches of Biéville, Rots, la Délivrande and Secqueville-en-Bessin (these latter two with wonderfully soaring spires), and the half-lost little Roman-esque church of Thaon, now deconsecrated and standing alone in its secret valley. There are splendid châteaux, too: Fontaine-Henry, built by the Harcourt family in the Renaissance style with an immensely tall roof; Lantheuil, dating from Louis XIII's reign, and Brécy, in the 17th-century Italianate style, all of which are open to visitors. Then there is Lasson, also Renais-sance, and Creullet, near Creully, in whose grounds General Montgomery parked his caravan headquarters during June of 1944. If there is still time after all this, one can see the former priory of St. Gabriel just west of Creully and then circle south-wards a bit, along some pretty, minor roads, past the fine abbey church of Mondaye and thence to **Balleroy**.

Perhaps one should spend a night here at the unassuming *Hôtel Restaurant du Marché*, leaving Balleroy itself and Cérisy, just west of it, for the following day. Then, having eaten the evening meal at the hotel, one can come back after a morning's sightseeing and lunch at the sumptuous *Manoir de la Drôme* restaurant hard by it. Or possibly one should combine these two places (and the lunch, of course) into a day out from Bayeux. However one arranges it, though, Balleroy should not be missed: the single street of the village was designed as part of the approach to the castle and frames it most admirably, while the château itself, designed by Mansart and set in gardens by Le Nôtre (of Versailles fame) is immensely rich inside.

It makes a perfect contrast to **Cérisy-la-Forêt**, on the other side of the great expanse of majestic beeches where deer and other wildlife roam, for Cérisy is of the utmost simplicity: an 11th-century abbey church in pale stone, with a few partly restored outbuildings, and one of the most stunning Romanesque monuments in Normandy.

Coming into **Bayeux** from here, one passes through the potters' village of Noron-la-Poterie, crosses the very efficient ring-road that keeps all through traffic out of town, and quickly finds oneself in front of the cathedral. This magnificent building, finished about a decade after the conquest of England under the supervision of William's pugnacious half-brother, the 'Fighting Bishop' Odo de Conteville, and the famous Bayeux Tapestry in the former Bishop's Palace nearby, so command the attention that one tends to ignore the rest of Bayeux. This is a pity, because as well as being the least damaged of all the Norman cities (it was captured, unscathed, on the day following D-Day), it also has one of the longest histories. A Gallo-Roman town, fought over by Bretons and Saxons as well as Normans, it provided Rollo, first Duke of

Normandy, with his wife, and was also the birthplace of his son and heir. It retained its Norse atmosphere (and language) for much longer than other Norman cities and it was here that Harold of England, returning from a fighting foray into Brittany in William's company, swore fealty to him with the oath he so quickly broke, unleashing the holocaust of Hastings.

Bayeux has charming and unspoiled old streets and mansions in the vicinity of the cathedral, a gem of an old hotel (the *Lion d'Or*, with gorgeous food) and an interesting museum in the old court house. But the cathedral itself is the focal point. Only the crypt, and the west front towers, remain from the original church, which Henry II's troops partially destroyed in the 12th century; appropriately, the tympanum of the south transept doorway shows scenes from the life of Thomas à Becket, Henry's murdered Archbishop of Canterbury.

It is the interior of the cathedral that most captivates me, however. The great nave and its side aisles are pure Romanesque, with wonderfully humorous grotesque carvings on the arches between the columns; above them rise high windows and vaulting that are 13th-century Gothic. The chancel is Romanesque, too; the superb choir stalls are late Gothic, and the marriage between the two styles is miraculous.

Down a little side street and across a courtyard, the famous tapestry is beautifully displayed in a specially designed room. This extraordinary mediaeval document, although known in French as the '*Tapisserie de la Reine Mathilde*', was probably made in England by order of Bishop Odo rather than Matilda. Considering the treatment to which it has been subjected down the centuries—at times bundled away out of sight; used as an aid to recruitment by Napoleon when planning his own invasion of England, and then, after Napoleon returned it to Bayeux in 1815, displayed there by unrolling (visitors were even allowed to finger it)—its condition is amazing. The last part is missing, and it has been restored in places, but it remains an extraordinarily vivid and convincing pictorial record.

North-west of Bayeux, **Formigny** is remembered for the battle in 1450 that finally drove the English out of Normandy; otherwise the coast beyond it is chiefly interesting for the operations that brought them back, with their allies, five hundred years later—nine centuries after the original Norman invasion. From the Orne to the Vire, the almost unbroken string of beaches, interrupted in a few places by low cliffs and backed by open pasturelands and wooded clumps, were the setting of one of the most intricate military operations of all time. The little seaside resorts along here are on the whole unremarkable, apart from Courseulles, of oyster fame, and the fishing village of Port-en-Bessin, which is not without charm; it is the Second World War associations that make them unique. The invasion has been fully enough chronicled elsewhere for those who want to re-trace it in detail, but even the most casual tourist would, I think, find it hard not to be stirred by the sight of the immaculately kept cemeteries, the monuments and pastel-painted kilometre stones, the beach names—Utah, Omaha, Gold, Juno, Sword—and, above all, by **Arromanches**. From the monument on the hillside just above it, there is a staggering view of the remains of the artificial port 'Mulberry B' which consisted of thousands of tons of concrete caissons, jetties and buoyant roadways, towed laboriously across the Channel to provide an invasion harbour on a coast where nothing adequate already existed. The first time I saw it, it was late on a grey and drizzly winter afternoon, and the hulks of the half-sunken concrete masses looked sinister enough against the pewtery sea to conjure up all sorts of visions of that June dawn in 1944. Damp and rather tired after a long day, I nevertheless drove down to the little seafront promenade to have a closer look, and then turned back towards the car. But a gnome-like figure darted at me from a nearby doorway. '*Mais vous n'avez pas vue la musée, Madame.*' I agreed I had not seen the museum, and started to explain that perhaps it was too late. Not at all, he insisted—for *une anglaise* to miss the museum was quite unthinkable, no matter what the hour: without the *anglais* there would never have been one. And so I had a solitary and moving conducted tour of all its models, photographs, plans and military impedimenta, and a private showing of the extremely realistic film, and had my proffered tip imperiously waved away.

The South

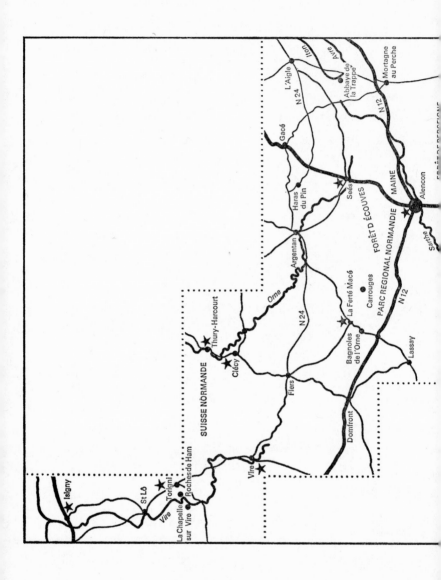

Southern Normandy is a mosaic of self-contained little regions, or *pays*, interspersed with forests and farmlands; anyone trying to cover the whole of Normandy in a limited time would find it hard to do justice to them all without following an impossibly convoluted course. Most lie on a fairly direct route between Paris and Brittany, though, and some can be crossed en route from the Channel ports either to Brittany or beyond.

The Perche country, south of the Pays d'Ouche, where the Avre and the Iton both rise to meander through a series of attractive lakelets, is the home of the majestic Percheron horse and wonderful riding country, with bridle paths threading the forests and a network of quiet lanes. Isolated in the Perche forest the monastery of La Grande Trappe, where the Trappist order was founded, may only be visited by men, so I merely pass on a friend's comment that its air of monastic sanctity is extraordinarily powerful and its architectural merits minimal.

Southwards by some 8 kilometres (5 miles) is the region's chief town, **Mortagne-au-Perche**, a not unattractive pattern of brownish-tiled roofs against the hillside on which it stands. I cannot work up any great enthusiasm for it, however, nor for Alençon, to the west. **Alençon** at least has the advantage of one superb restaurant (*Petit Vatel*) which is within walking distance of its flamboyant Gothic church (fine 16th-century stained glass), so it makes a convenient lunch stop. It has two other claims to fame, as well, one possibly apocryphal. This is the story that, when Duke William was besieging it during his pre-Conquest subjugation of Normandy, the citizens draped the ramparts with animal skins to remind him that his mother was merely a tanner's daughter. William supposedly made them pay dearly for this impudence—by severing the hands and feet of the thirty prisoners he held, and sending the gruesome proof of his anger into the town for all to see. Alençon's second claim to fame is as a lace-making centre, thanks to the acumen of Louis XIV's minister Colbert, born at Rouen, who served his native Normandy as well as he served his king: when Venetian lace came into fashion in the mid-17th century, he set up competitive industries in Alençon and in Argentan. One can see examples of old Alençon lace in the Musée de Peinture, and both see and buy the modern variety at the Lace School in the rue du Pont-Neuf, leading to the bridge across the Sarthe.

South-east of Alençon is the Perseigne forest, surprisingly little frequented, while to the south-west the Sarthe valley, popular with anglers, winds down to the oddly named Alpes Mancelles—an unduly grandiose name for the escarpments that frame the river's course. More interesting, to my mind, is the country north of Alençon: the beautifully kept Forest of Ecouves, with its tidy piles of logs and its network of marked paths for walkers. One can drive through it too, of course, past the Croix de Médavy crossroads, where a French tank commemorates General Leclerc's mopping-up operations in the summer of 1944, and then turning off to look at the enormous Château of **Carrouges**. This stands in a peculiar situation below the hilltop village (of the same name) where the original Norman fortress was, but the ensemble, with its chequered brickwork, is extremely striking; the Renaissance gateway flanked by twin towers leading to the moated castle beyond. The Lords of Carrouges ruled this region from as far back as the 12th century; one was ambassador to England in the 17th century and instrumental in arranging the marriage between Louis XII's sister Henrietta Maria and the future Charles I. The castle now belongs to the State and can be visited.

From Carrouges one can come back across the Ecouves

forest to **Sées,** a serious little town with a nice market square on the north side of its lovely, miniature, early Gothic cathedral. It has other merits: an impressive former Bishop's Palace, the ruins of the Romanesque church of St. Pierre nicely placed opposite the agreeable, simple *Hôtel Restaurant du Cheval Blanc;* a graceful former 18th-century abbey (St. Martin), and the Notre-Dame church, with 16th-century bas-reliefs.

Between Sées and Argentan, winding along the side roads in an easterly curve, there are all sorts of things to see: the romantic-looking moated Château d'O and its more severe-looking neighbour, the Château de Médavy; the bulky church of Almenêches, and the stud farm of Haras du Pin, another useful gift from Colbert to Normandy which now houses some of the finest stallions in France in buildings whose core was designed by Mansart. Lovely satiny horses, their paddocks bordered with neat white fences, are to be seen all over the Pays d'Argentan, in fact; pony-minded children go mad with excitement at the sight of them. Beyond the Haras du Pin is Exmès, one-time capital of the area; coming into Argentan from this direction one can take in two more châteaux: le Bourg-St. Leonard, long and low and pale, and Chambois, a vast 12th-century keep with round, conical-hatted towers at each corner. Here it was that the Battle of Normandy ended, in August 1944.

Argentan itself, badly damaged in the preceding battles, is nonetheless a pleasant enough little town; it has two interesting churches (St. Germain and St. Martin), the remains of a 14th-century castle across the square from St. Germain, and a nice market place. It was here, incidentally, that Henry II of England uttered the fateful phrase 'Will nobody rid me of this turbulent priest?' that led to Thomas à Becket's murder in 1170.

South and east of Argentan, **La Ferté Macé** is both a lively market town and a spa, but is better known for its special recipe for *tripes en brochette*; if one is lucky, it may be on the menu at the *Auberge de Clouet* or at the *Grand Turc*—at either of which I would happily stay for a night or two. As a spa, it is eclipsed by nearby **Bagnoles de l'Orne**, well-manicured, surrounded by woodlands, and redolent of the intense concentration the French devote to anything concerning their health. It has dozens of hotels, which make it an alternative (though to my mind less amusing) stopping place, and from here one can loop south to a trio of castles: picturesque Couterne, in the forest on the outskirts of Bagnoles; redoubtable Lassay, a masterpiece of 15th-century military architecture, with no fewer than eight, fat, brownish-gold towers enclosing a series of courtyards, and ruined Bois-Thibault just to the north of it. And from here anyone as fascinated by castles as I am has only 16 kilometres (10 miles) more to negotiate for **Domfront**, even more spectacular, piled above the gorge of the Varenne. Although only two massive sections of the keep remain standing at one end of the town, this former frontier-fortress, built by the pugnacious Bellêmes in the 11th century, is oddly evocative. Formal gardens surround the ruins and the street alongside is called rue Montgomery; this and the splashes of red salvia and begonia are reminders that the unfortunate Captain Montgomery of the Scots Guards was executed here on Catherine de Medici's orders. He had had the ill luck to have made her a widow (and simultaneously robbed Diane de Poitiers of her lover) by mortally wounding Henri II in a jousting match. It was here too, incidentally, that the other Henry II (of England) learned of the penance imposed upon him by the Pope for the murder of Thomas à Becket—to walk barefoot to Canterbury and be scourged by the monks there.

Directly north of Domfront is **Flers**, with yet another castle (now the Town Hall) standing in a park on a bend of the Vire that serves it both as a moat and a lake. And north of that again is the region known as the Suisse Normande. 'Norman Switzerland', however, is a silly misnomer that conveys nothing of this gentle, picture-book country of secret valleys and velvety hills, bright in springtime with gorse and broom, where the villages are of glowing pinkish stone and lonely chapels stand sentinel on the hilltops. It is a paradise for walkers, with marked walks of varying length and difficulty, and on the occasional rocky escarpments of the Orne youngsters practise rock-climbing—which is about the nearest association it has with Switzerland. **Clécy** (the *Relais de Surosne* hotel), Pont d'Ouilly and **Thury-Harcourt** (make a mental note of the *Relais de la Poste* here) are the main tourist centres of this attractive countryside, which abounds in viewpoints, streams, woods, pastures and picnic places.

Bordering on the Suisse Normande is the area around Vire, a network of little valleys that wrinkle the green *bocage* woodlands. **Vire** itself, though almost entirely modern, is the place in which to eat *andouilles*—rich black chitterling sausages; try the *Cheval Blanc* or the *des Voyageurs* for them. The Place du Château, with the ruins of an early 12th-century keep on a hilltop, has wonderful views across the valleys (Vaux de Vire, from which the word 'vaudeville' is said to have come—by way of a 15th-century folk singer). Below this square the badly damaged Notre-Dame church has now been virtually rebuilt in its original early Gothic style; beyond this again is a large new square with the ancient town gateway and belfry as its focal point.

Following the Vire valley northwards, **La Chapelle-sur-Vire** has been a place of pilgrimage since the 12th century, and old sculptures have been incorporated into the simple 19th-century church there. Slightly further north the **Rocher de Ham** is a celebrated viewpoint, and **Torigni-sur-Vire**, just east of it, a pleasant little town with a vast château (rebuilt after the Second World War) on the central market square, has a nice small hotel, the Orangerie.

And so to **St. Lô**, still on the Vire but no longer really in southern Normandy; a transition point between it and the Cotentin. The Ruskins spent a week there, rowing on the river, admiring the 'fine old Norman château among the trees', the church, and the old houses, and having innumerable baths, to their great delight, at a bathing house. Alas for this ancient city, once a Gaulish settlement and renamed in the 6th century, for it was reduced to rubble in one of the fiercest battles of the Second World War. Only parts of the ramparts remained, and the decapitated towers and west front (now partly restored) of Notre-Dame church; the rest is entirely new. But it has been happily planned and its people are delighted with it; they go out of their way to point out anything they feel should not be missed. A good lady with a string bag full of carrots and turnips steered me to the 'new' Romanesque church of Ste. Croix, rebuilt from its original materials, and urged me to venture further out in the same direction to see the stud farm. This, together with the hospital (partly American-financed) and the excellent little museum in the new Town Hall, are the pride and joy of a particularly friendly citizenry.

One more brief halt before the Contentin peninsula: at **Isigny**, towards the mouth of the Vire. Not 'sur mer', as its name implies, it is a favourite stop of mine because it is not only a cream and butter centre but is also the heart of the famous *pré salé* country—the salt meadows that give so distinctive a taste to the young stock, particularly lambs, grazing upon them. A tour of the Isigny Dairy Cooperative followed by lunch in one of its small hotel-restaurants (the *France* and the *Commerce*, almost next door to one another) is an excellent prelude to the Cotentin proper.

The Cotentin
Mont-St. Michel and
its Approaches

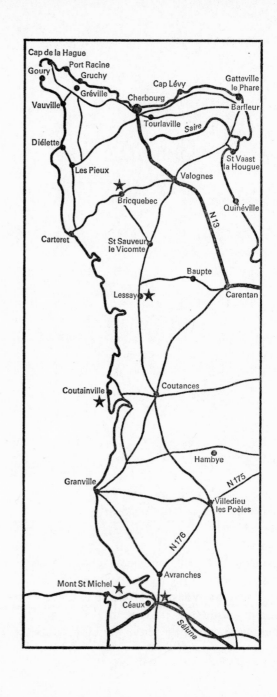

Crossing the Vire, one is on the lowest lying part of an irregularly shaped peninsula whose tip was in ancient times an island. Behind the undulating sand-dunes of Utah beach stretch endless marshy meadows full of dairy herds and criss-crossed by the hedgerows and sunken roads that so hampered the American advance in 1944. Since Napoleon's time there have been plans to drain these marshes; he himself toyed with the idea of cutting a navigable canal through them, but no major schemes have emerged apart from the development of the peat industry around Baupte. One can see the spire of Carentan's Notre-Dame church from miles away across this flat and featureless countryside; the town itself, entirely cattle and dairy orientated, where only a handful of the buildings still stand, comes as something of an anti-climax. But it is a good departure point for an anti-clockwise circuit of the Cotentin, starting with the excellent Utah Beach Museum, dedicated to the American forces.

A minor road runs north behind the dunes to Quinéville, from which one can look across to the anchorage of St. Vaast. Here in 1692 an Irish-Catholic army assembled to join Louis XIV's French fleet and restore the deposed Catholic monarch, James II, to the English throne. But the French ships, coming from Brest, were intercepted by an Anglo-Dutch force off Barfleur and a four-day battle ensued (La Hougue) which ended with a large part of the French fleet being burned to the waterlines. All this James II was able to see from a vantage point at Quinéville, and he is said to have wept as the ships, and his last hope of the throne, went up in smoke.

Today **St. Vaast-la-Hougue** is a pretty little resort famous for its oysters; its port, with a small sailors' chapel near the landward end of the jetty, was built well after the battle. And the beach which stretches away to the south of it softens the stern lines of the Fort de la Hougue, still a military base, at the tip of a narrow spit of land.

Inland of St. Vaast lies the enchanting green valley of the Saire, speckled with stone hamlets and farmhouses—a foretaste of the Armorican regions of the Cotentin further west, and of Brittany. To the north, past the aristocratic manor house of La Crasvillerie, is the fishing village-cum-resort of **Barfleur**, once an important port for Anglo-Norman traffic, off which sank, in 1120, the ship carrying Henry I's only son and a hundred of his companions.

At Barfleur one can go on north to the Gatteville lighthouse for some splendid views of the coast, or cut inland slightly, via the nice little village of St. Pierre-Eglise which has a church with a fine Romanesque doorway, and an 18th-century castle, and rejoin the coast later, at the Cap Lévy lighthouse. The corniche road from here to Bretteville, just short of Cherbourg, unrolls a series of magnificent views, sending the *Green Michelin Guide* into transports of enthusiasm tempered with a cautious warning to 'drive slowly to enjoy the full beauty of the trip'.

By Bretteville I have had enough of views, and prefer to turn inland for the Château de Tourlaville. A majestic Renaissance mansion in a beautiful park, it is bound up with a strange and tragic story of a young brother and sister of amazing beauty who grew up here, fell incestuously in love, and were finally executed for their crime in Paris, where they had fled, in 1603. Thinking of this imparts a melancholy aura to the beautifully kept gardens around the château, where youngsters from Cherbourg come to stroll or play among the trees and beside the pools.

Cherbourg has an even longer history than Le Havre: it was founded early in the 13th century by Philippe-Auguste of France, soon after he had conquered the Duchy of Normandy. But it seems to have had scant attention paid to it thereafter until the military architect, Vauban, started fortifications in 1686, and then it was neglected again for nearly a century until work on the great breakwater began. Unsuccessful at first, the installations being destroyed by the sea almost as fast as they were put in place, the sunken foundations eventually caused the sea itself to build up rocky deposits, and on top of these the breakwater finally took shape in 1853. Napoleon III continued the work and the first transatlantic liner sailed from Cherbourg in 1869, twelve years after Queen Victoria's visit to mark the inauguration of the railway from Caen.

The old port was blasted to pieces in 1944, of course; when the Americans finally took Cherbourg at the end of June they found the harbour blocked with sunken ships. But in less than two months it was sufficiently cleared for the submarine pipeline PLUTO to start bringing fuel from England's Isle of Wight to the invading forces. Some idea of the scale of this operation can be gained from a visit to the Fort du Roule Invasion Museum, a splendid viewpoint.

The other museum worth visiting is the one in the Town Hall which has canvases and drawings by Millet, Cotentin-bred and unequalled in his portrayals of rural Norman life. Behind this museum and to the east of it, up to the quayside of the inner port, are the most characteristic and lively streets of present-day Cherbourg; also several good little restaurants.

West of Cherbourg stretches the wild and rocky **Cap de la Hague**, with a big atomic power station tucked into one of its valleys. The best views are from the rugged, jagged, gorse-covered cliffs of the southern coast, from the Nez de Jobourg across the wicked Alderney Race currents; the north coast is curiously domesticated in appearance, with huge hydrangea hedges. At Gruchy, almost at the sea's edge on the north coast, one can see the house in which Millet was born; the church at nearby Gréville figures in several of his paintings. Towards the tip of the peninsula, en route to Goury, Port-

Racine (with a perfectly charming little hotel nearby) is said to be France's smallest port, and Goury, strategically situated for victims of the Alderney currents, probably has one of its busiest lifeboat stations.

South of the Nez de Jobourg, Vauville has a cosy little church and a manor house overlooked by the one-time priory of St. Hermel; Diélette is a nice little port with a good beach and the park of the castle of Flamanville just south of it; Carteret is a popular resort from which boats ply back and forth to Jersey.

Inland of this stretch of coast, a pretty road leads to **Bricquebec**, famous for its Trappist monastery but perhaps even more interesting for the remains of its huge 14th-century castle which Queen Victoria visited after the celebrations at Cherbourg in 1857. Now laid out with flowerbeds and lawns, it also incorporates a particularly pleasant small hotel-restaurant. East of Bricquebec, a little detour brings one to **Valognes** via the Château of Chiffrevast and some lovely countryside, and though Valognes today is largely a modern dairy and market town, there are still a few traces to be found of the era when it was the self-styled social capital of the Cotentin. Here and there an old mansion reminds one that Valognes was once crammed with such dwellings, boasting a 'high society' whose absurdities were satirised by the author of *Gil Blas* and more kindly chronicled by the 19th-century Cotentin novelist Barbey d'Aurevilly—he who left an account of Beau Brummell's last days at Caen.

Barbey d'Aurevilly's home town was **St. Sauveur-le-Vicomte**, 26 kilometres (about 16 miles) south of Valognes, and he lived there until the end of an ill-fated affair with a married woman drove him to Paris and journalism. But his roots remained in the Cotentin and his novels are steeped in Norman atmosphere, particularly the folklore and superstitions of the Cotentin. The castle of St. Sauveur, ruined though it was during 1944, is still imposing-looking, and contains a small museum of the writer's belongings; he is buried in the grounds. There is also an interesting 14th-century statue of St. James of Compostela in the church.

Barbey d'Aurevilly also immortalised the Ste. Croix Fair which takes place at **Lessay** in mid-September and is one of the most important of Norman festivals. Never having managed to be there at the right time, I cannot elaborate, but no one should miss Lessay, for its abbey church is not just one of the finest examples of Romanesque art in Normandy but holds its own among all the Romanesque buildings of France. Its proportions, enhanced by simplicity of detail, are superb and the delicately muted, modern, stained-glass windows admirably complement the whole. There is every inducement to linger there, too, for the particularly agreeable *Hostellerie de l'Abbaye* makes a delightful overnight stop. Thus one can not only do Lessay justice but also compare it with the cathedral at **Coutances**, 21 kilometres (about 13 miles) to the south. This astonishing building, the largest in the region, was originally built in Romanesque style in the mid-11th century, largely from money contributed by the three redoubtable de Hautevilles, Normans from the village of Hauteville le Guichard, between Coutances and St. Lô. They were the Norman kings of Apulia and Sicily, and the founder of Coutances, Geoffroy de Montbray, toiled all the way out to the Mediterranean to solicit funds for his church. A century and a half later, however, it burned down, and a Gothic cathedral was built on its remains. Ruskin, having at first sight compared it rather slightingly to Salisbury, ended by conceding that it was 'a pure and complete example of the very earliest French Gothic' and its facade, in particular, is a paean of vertical lines—tapered windows and candle-like towers—culminating in slender twin spires. The simple, octagonal lantern tower is equally impressive, and the soaring simplicity of the interior matches that of the west front. For those with a head for heights, a tour of the upper parts culminates in a spectacular view from the top of the lantern tower, extending on a clear day as far as Jersey. One might, though, add that it rather disinclines one from exploring the rest of the town, which is rebuilt on less inspiring lines.

Coutances's nearest seaside resort is **Coutainville**, an unassuming little place that nonetheless has one modest hotel (the *Hardy*) with very good food. This alone makes me prefer it to **Granville**, further south, though Granville has been a resort for far longer—since the mid-19th century, in fact—and is far livelier. More interesting still, however, is to go inland from Coutances, first to the Abbaye de **Hambye** and then to **Villedieu-les-Poëles** (literally, 'God's frying-pan town') where a solemn procession on the third Sunday after Whitsun every four years (the next is in 1979) commemorates the foundation here in the 12th century of the first headquarters of the Knights of St. John.

The ruins of Hambye are difficult to find, hidden in the tiny valley of the Seine, but are worth seeking: past a thatched gateway overgrown with irises, the ruins of a vast Gothic church, patched with lichens in varying shades of ochre, glow warmly in the shadows. Some of the monastic buildings are almost in their original state and partly furnished with old pieces and hangings, and the literature the caretaker lends to visitors traces the abbey's connections with Great Massingham, in Norfolk.

One is very close here to Villedieu, whose present name has nothing to do with the Knights of St. John but dates from the 17th century, when its copper craftsmen supplied the farms of Normandy with their milk cans. There are some nice little side streets and courtyards to explore, but the main street is marred by shops ablaze with copper, mostly ugly souvenirs. Not everything is brash and nasty, though: I once spotted a charming coal hod, old-fashioned in design and not too burnished for my taste. But it was Sunday and I was short of cash, so the maker agreed, with many affirmations of faith in British honesty, to take an English cheque. Then—probably as further proof of his trust, but rather as though I had proposed to undress—he pointedly turned his back and looked the other way while I wrote it.

The attractive ruins of another former abbey, La Lucerne, are nearer to the Granville road than to the Villedieu one, but are roughly in the direction of Avranches, at the innermost point of the bay of Mont-St. Michel. Avranches already existed in the 6th century, when thick woods grew around it and Mont-St. Michel (then called Mont Tombe) rose from treetops rather than sand-flats. Its countryside was still forested when St. Aubert was its Bishop in 708, and received a visitation from the Archangel Michael who asked why there was no chapel to him on the top of the mount. (Chapels to St. Michael were often built on summits then, just as in Greece today the highest hilltop shrines are usually dedicated to the Prophet Elijah.) Bishop Aubert apparently dismissed the vision as a mere dream, and similarly disbelieved the authenticity of a subsequent apparition. At the third visit St. Michael became impatient and emphasised his command by tapping the Bishop forcefully on the head with one finger. This made a hole in Aubert's head which galvanised him to action and his skull, with a hole in it, is the somewhat grisly principal exhibit in the treasury of St. Gervais' basilica.

The original Cathedral of **Avranches**, pulled down at the end of the 18th century because it had become unsafe, was where Henry II of England knelt to receive Papal absolution for the murder of Thomas à Becket, and the spot is marked by a paving stone set in a high-perched square at the edge of town. Despite its lack of a cathedral today I still find it an attractive town, particularly as it was unscathed by the Second World War; General Patton's American troops, beginning from here their crushing advance in August 1944, moved so fast that there was no destruction.

The shortest way from Avranches to Mont-St. Michel is along a minor road that crosses the salt marshes and passes, at **Céaux**, the delightful little *Au P'tit Quinquin* hotel.

The views of the mount, rising from its grey sand-flats, are marvellous from whichever direction one approaches it, though Ruskin was disappointed by the colour of the sand 'channelled by brown and stinking rivulets' and by the fact that some of the buildings were still used as a prison. But even Ruskin had to admit that the ensemble was picturesque, and the drama of the setting is quite breathtaking. However, the effect can be marred at the peak of the tourist or pilgrimage season, when one arrives at the end of the causeway to find the car parks full and the place thronged with people, though this is perhaps a selfish reaction to a place that has been a venerated shrine to pilgrims for over a thousand years.

Bishop Aubert's original oratory was soon replaced by an abbey, and from then on succeeding generations piled increasingly splendid buildings upon the mount. The early Normans treated it with great respect and atoned handsomely for the damage their marauding forebears had done to it, raising a Romanesque abbey above the Carolingian church (now known as Notre-Dame-sous-Terre) where William the Conqueror's grandfather married Judith of Brittany. The Gothic abbey, and the wonderful la Merveille buildings, were largely financed by Philippe-Auguste of France after he in his turn had battered the shrine during his 13th-century Normandy battles. Other buildings continued to be added until the early 16th century, and all the while pilgrims flocked there—purchasing special passes from the English when they held the surrounding region during the Hundred Years War—patronising the souvenir shops that even then abounded, and packing the place almost as tightly as they do today.

Selfish or not, however, I still prefer to go there in winter or in early spring when I can wander through its maze-like buildings at my own pace and un-jostled, and the commercialism of establishments that line the steep Grande Rue is not quite so blatant. It involves a slight sacrifice: since my first and only high-season visit, when the *Mère Poularde* restaurant was too crowded even to contemplate, I have never been there when it was open, so have never sampled one of its famous fluffy omelettes. But there are compensations. One has time and space to notice the detail: the different-coloured types of granite (from the Chausey Islands and Brittany) used so effectively in the abbey church, and the contrast between its Romanesque nave and Gothic chancel. Going out into the exquisite little cloister that forms part of the la Merveille complex, one really does feel suspended between earth and sky if there are no crowds, and alone in the refectory the pale luminosity coming through the *grisaille* glass, set deep into the slim Gothic side embrasures, feels almost unearthly. Those two structures, the cloister and the refectory, together with the graceful *Salle des Hôtes* below them, are for me the climax of Mont-St. Michel: after threading my way through the *Salle des Chevaliers* and a series of crypts, eerie when quite empty, it is a relief to emerge on to the ramparts. Gazing out to sea, one then starts to brood about this extraordinary shrine: about the feats of engineering that the raising of the buildings must have involved, even though the sea had not encroached so far during the early stages of construction; about the laziness of the late 16th-century incumbents who allowed it to start slipping into decline; about the heedless Revolutionaries who transformed part of it into the penal settlement that so horrified the Ruskins; and about the latter-day restorers who have perhaps occasionally allowed their zeal to outstrip the bounds of good taste—but have not, even so, managed to eclipse its unique character.

Norman Cuisine

NOTES ON RECIPES AND MEASUREMENTS

I have tried to choose recipes that give the authentic flavour of the region but are neither too expensive nor too complicated to make. Sometimes the choice has also been influenced not only by what family and friends can reasonably be asked to eat, but also by the fact that many traditionally cheap and ubiquitous French ingredients, particularly fish, are not so easy to lay hands on elsewhere. Sometimes I have given alternatives (i.e. gammon for *jambon du pays*).

There are, however, certain things every cook must have to hand if the authentic flavours are to be reproduced. A wide variety of herbs is one, including sorrel (which is very easy to grow, even in a window box, and comes up without fuss year after year). Garlic is another, and so are peppercorns and a mill to grind them in, and so is unsalted butter. *Crème fraîche* is another essential and delicious element of many regional dishes, and this can be made very easily by combining two parts of ordinary double cream with one part of commercially soured cream and leaving it, covered with a cloth, at room temperature for four hours or more to 'take'. After this, it can be stored in the refrigerator for a week or ten days if necessary.

On the subject of wines, I have deliberately been non-committal since I am no expert. There are plenty of excellent wine-guides to which the more discerning reader can refer; for my own part, I am quite happy to ask for what is local in restaurants, the *vin du pays*, and to let the *patron* or *patronne* advise me which particular one, if there are alternatives, would best suit the food I am to eat. One rarely goes wrong using this method in honest French restaurants; in the recipes, except where a special liquor is called for, I have either named the wine originally specified, if it can be obtained easily and cheaply outside France, or simply indicated a general type of wine, such as 'dry red'.

Throughout the recipes, I have mostly quoted metric weights and measurements, occasionally using the widely accepted 'tablespoon' and 'teaspoon' when they seemed more relevant. New scales that show both grammes and ounces, and especially the new measuring jugs marked off in millilitres as well as fluid ounces, are a great help to the non-metrically-minded cook, but as an additional aid two tables of rough equivalents are given. Oven temperatures are already quoted in Centigrade, Fahrenheit and Gas Marks in the individual recipes to which they apply. And quantities, unless otherwise stated, are for six people throughout.

LIQUID MEASUREMENTS (APPROXIMATE)

French	English	American
1 cl (10 gr)	⅓ fl oz	1 dessertspoon
1 dl (100 gr)	3½ fl oz	Just under ¼ cup
¼ litre (250 gr)	About 9 fl oz	Just over 1 cup
½ litre (500 gr)	About 18 fl oz	About 2¼ cups
1 litre (1000 gr)	About 35 fl oz or 1¾ pints	Just over 4¼ cups

SOLID MEASUREMENTS (APPROXIMATE)

25 gr	Just under an ounce	About 2 tbsps (level) of fat or sugar; about 4 tbsps flour

50 gr	Slightly under 2 oz	Just under ¼ cup of fat or sugar; double that of flour
100 gr	3½ oz	Just under ½ cup fat or sugar; a scant cup of flour
250 gr	About 9 oz	Slightly over a cup of fat or sugar; 2¼ cups flour
500 gr ('une livre')	1.1 lb	2 cups fat; 2¼ cups sugar; 4½ cups flour
1 kg (1000 gr)	2.2 lbs	4 cups fat; 4½ cups sugar; 9 cups flour

Abbreviations used throughout:

ml = millilitre;	cl = centilitre;
dl = decilitre;	gr = gramme(s);
kg = kilogramme;	tsp = level teaspoonful (5 ml);
tbsp = level tablespoonful (20 ml)	

The bases of Norman cooking, as I have said, are cream, thick and satiny (and sweet, as opposed to the faintly 'sour' *crème fraîche* that is also sometimes used), unsalted butter, cider, and Calvados. To get top quality cream outside Normandy, and rural areas elsewhere, can be a problem, but the addition of an egg yolk to the heaviest varieties sold in the average super-market often helps. It is more difficult to get cider that is really dry and not too fizzy—and, of course, Calvados. I would therefore urge people to bring some Calvados home: a bottle goes a long way, and it need not be the most expensive variety; also a sample of good Normandy *cidre bouché* so that it can be used as a basis of comparison with varieties available at home.

I am indebted to Monsieur Julien Nicolle, Mayor of Mont-St. Michel, for help over some of the following recipes; he it was who introduced me to the excellent Flammarion volume on Norman cooking.* The quantities, incidentally, unless otherwise stated, are for six people.

Potage Avranchinais

This is a very simple recipe—at first sight, almost too simple—but to people who have fallen into the 'convenience soup' habit it can come as a revelation.

Ingredients

1½ kg firm tomatoes
3 or 4 onions, according to size
1 clove of garlic
1 bouquet garni (parsley, bayleaf, thyme and a stick of cinnamon)

2½ dl cream
1 good knob of butter
1 tablespoon flour
salt and pepper
1¼ litre water

Method

Chop the onions and the skinned tomatoes and soften them gently in the melted butter for 15 minutes or so, stirring occasionally. Add the sliced garlic clove and sprinkle with the flour. Stir and cook gently for five more minutes. Add both the water and the bouquet garni, stir until it comes to the boil, then cover and leave to simmer for about half an hour. Rub through a sieve (or liquidise in a blender and strain). Reserve one soup-ladleful and return the rest to the saucepan. Season lightly with salt and freshly ground pepper and re-heat gently. Meantime, put the cream at the bottom of a warm soup tureen or deep earthenware dish and, if it is not very thick, whisk an egg yolk

* *Gastronomie Normande d'hier et d'aujourd'hui* by Simone Morand (Flammarion).

into it. Stir in the reserved ladleful of now cool soup and then add the rest gradually, stirring continually.

Soupe à l'Oseille

Ingredients

Two good fistfuls of sorrel leaves

4 egg yolks

2 dl cream

1½ litres water or light-flavoured stock made of poultry or game

2 tablespoons butter

2 tablespoons flour

salt

pepper

Method

Wash the sorrel leaves and strip off the thickest parts of the stalks, dry them, and cut into thin strips (easily done with kitchen scissors if the leaves are arranged and held in an orderly bunch). Soften the sorrel gently in the melted butter, add the flour and blend. Add water or stock, stirring constantly. Bring to boil slowly and season. Reserve one ladleful of the soup and simmer the rest for 10–12 minutes. Blend the cream and the egg yolks in the bottom of a slightly warmed soup tureen or deep earthenware dish, stir in the ladleful of reserved soup and then pour in the rest when still only just off the boil, in a steady stream, stirring constantly. May be kept warm in the oven, but must not boil again.

Salade du Pêcheur

This is a useful hors d'oeuvre for a dinner party, as it can be made the previous day and kept refrigerated. It is, in fact, better flavoured if made in advance.

Ingredients

1 onion, chopped	4 litres mussels
1 shallot, chopped	oil
1 bouquet garni of thyme,	vinegar
bayleaf, parsley and dill	salt
½ litre dry cider	pepper
½ litre water	chopped fresh parsley

Method

Make a *court-bouillon* by simmering the onion, shallot and bouquet garni in the cider and water for 20–30 minutes and then let it cool while preparing the mussels, cleaning and scraping them thoroughly and rinsing in cold water. Put the mussels in a large pan, pour the tepid court-bouillon over them, cover closely and heat gently without boiling, shaking the pan once or twice, until the mussels have opened their shells and are cooked (8–10 minutes). Remove mussels from their shells and put in a bowl, meanwhile reducing the court-bouillon to about ¼ litre and allowing it to cool. Make a dressing of oil, salt, pepper, the reduced court-bouillon and a touch of vinegar to taste, pour it over the mussels and shake until all are well steeped in it. Cover and refrigerate as long as is convenient, and serve in individual dishes topped with chopped parsley.

Sole au Cidre
(for 4)

Ingredients

1 large, thick fresh sole,	enough dry cider to cover
cleaned but left whole	most of the fish (about
2 finely chopped shallots	¼ litre)
8–10 branches of parsley,	butter
chopped	salt and pepper

Method

Lay the sole in a buttered oven dish, sprinkle with salt and freshly ground black pepper. Distribute the shallots and most of the parsley around it and pour on the cider. (If a sizeable part of the fish remains uncovered, lay a sheet of tinfoil lightly over it for the first 15 minutes of cooking; there should not be too much liquid.) Put in a pre-heated oven (160°C, 325°F, or gas mark 3) for 25–30 minutes according to the size of the fish. Sprinkle the rest of the parsley over the top before serving.

Turbot de Courseulles-sur-Mer

Ingredients

1 litre white wine court-bouillon made well in advance by the method described below	3 dl thick cream
	35 gr butter
	25 gr flour
	2 or 3 egg yolks, according to the thickness of the cream
1 good-sized turbot (or brill), cleaned and cut crosswise into thick steaks	
	salt
1 tin asparagus tips	pepper

Method (1)

Make the court-bouillon by combining equal quantities of water and white wine, adding a bouquet garni, a medium-sized onion and four medium-sized carrots cut into rounds, a shallot stuck with three cloves, coarse salt and some fresh-ground black pepper, and boiling it, covered, for half an hour or so. Leave to cool.

Method (2)

Arrange the fish steaks closely together in a shallow saucepan and strain the cold court-bouillon over them. They should be entirely covered. Cover and heat very gently, allowing the surface of the liquid to shiver but not to simmer. When cooked through but still quite firm (err on the side of under-cooking), remove from liquid, arrange on a serving dish, surround with the asparagus tips and put in a low oven to keep warm. Make a roux of the butter and flour and stir in a half-litre of the cooking liquid. When it has boiled for a few minutes, remove and reserve a soup-ladleful and allow the remainder to continue cooking, stirring from time to time, until reduced by nearly a half. Meantime, beat the egg yolks lightly in a bowl and gently blend in first the cooled ladleful of sauce and then the cream. Pour this mixture in a thin, steady stream into the boiling sauce, stirring briskly, and then cover the fish with it. It will come to no harm if kept in a low oven for 15 minutes or so before serving.

Tripes à la mode de Caen

A homelier version of one of the classic Norman dishes, it can be appreciated in my experience even by people who profess an antipathy to offal.

Ingredients

1 generous kg tripe, cleaned and blanched
350 gr onions
350 gr leeks
6–8 carrots
200 gr bacon rind
1 pig's trotter (or, ideally, 2 calves' feet, but these can be difficult to get)
2 or 3 cloves garlic

1 shallot stuck with two cloves
½ litre cider
1 wineglass Calvados
bouquet garni
salt
pepper
pinch of cumin
flour-and-water paste

Method

Use an oven dish with a well-fitting lid, earthenware for preference but any heavy-bottomed casserole will do, and lay the rough-chopped pig's trotter, bacon rind and garlic at the bottom and cover with half the vegetables, cut into rounds. Sprinkle with salt, pepper and cumin; place the shallot at the centre and cover with half the tripe, cut into 5-cm squares. Repeat with another layer of vegetables, seasoning, and another of tripe. Pour on the cider and Calvados. If the dish is not quite full, cover closely with a sheet of foil and press it down gently on the ingredients. Seal the lid into place with a flour-and-water paste and cook in a low oven (140°C, 275°F, or gas mark 1) for about 9–10 hours.

Poulet Vallée d'Auge

There are several variations on this classic chicken dish, this one being probably the simplest to prepare.

Ingredients

1 good-sized fresh chicken (not frozen), cut into 6 serving pieces	3 dl thick cream
	knob of butter
	1 soup-ladleful of Calvados
250 gr streaky bacon	salt and pepper
6 finely chopped shallots	

Method

Lay the chicken pieces in a roasting pan, skin upwards, and rub lightly with a slice of lemon. Put one or two small pieces of bacon on each, using about half the bacon. Roast in a moderately hot oven (190°C, 375°F, or gas mark 5) for about 15–20 minutes, or until the pieces are cooked through and the juices run clear when pricked. Meantime, cut the rest of the bacon into slivers, put to cook gently in butter and add the chopped shallots. Stir until the shallots are soft, add the cream, stir, and allow to heat thoroughly while removing the chicken pieces from the oven and flaming them with the Calvados. Transfer chicken pieces to a serving dish and keep warm. Stir the cream sauce into the cooking juices, scraping the pan well, and then strain the sauce over the chicken pieces. Return the dish to the oven (10 minutes at 190°C, 375F°, or gas mark 5; lower if it is convenient to leave it longer). Serve with plain rice.

Epaule de Mouton à la Crème

Ingredients

1 shoulder of lamb or
  mutton on the bone
marinade composed of
  1 litre very dry cider,
  1 wineglass Calvados, 1 teaspoon cider vinegar, 1 teaspoon oil, 1 large onion
  cut into rounds, 1 chopped
  garlic clove, 2 cloves, 1
  bouquet garni comprising
  rosemary, bayleaf, parsley
  1 teaspoon salt, freshly
  ground black pepper

2 tablespoons butter
2 tablespoons or more of
  flour
2 dl double cream
2 dl soured cream
2 egg yolks
salt
freshly ground black pepper

Method

Combine the marinade ingredients in a large heavy-duty polythene bag. Trim as much surplus fat as possible off the shoulder of lamb and put it into the marinade. Exclude sufficient air so that the joint is entirely surrounded by marinade and stand in a dish in the refrigerator for at least 12 hours. Remove the joint and dry it with kitchen paper or a clean cloth; brown it well on both sides in butter in a broad heavy pan. When nicely browned, up-end the joint at one side of the pan and gradually stir in enough flour to absorb all the fat. Strain the marinade liquid into a jug and add gradually to the flour mixture, stirring until smooth. Replace joint upside down and cook over a low flame for ¾ hour. Turn and cook for another ¾ hour. Remove pan from heat, take out joint and leave on a carving board to set for 15 minutes while the cooking liquid cools. Blend egg yolks, sour cream and sweet cream together in a bowl. Carve as much lamb as needed from the joint and arrange on an oven-proof dish and put in very low oven to keep warm. Skim excess fat from cooking liquid and pour in the egg and cream mixture, whisking steadily. Add more salt and pepper to taste and re-heat gently without boiling. Pour over meat and leave in low oven for up to half an hour to allow flavours to blend. Serve with plain boiled potatoes or rice.

Faisan à la Normande

Ingredients

1 brace pheasants
1 wineglass Calvados
butter
1¾ kg cooking apples
¼ kg tart dessert apples
    (Granny Smith or green
    Golden Delicious)

¼ litre double cream and
    soured cream, in equal
    proportions
salt
pepper

Method

Melt a good knob of butter in a heavy saucepan or cast-iron enamelled dish large enough to hold the pheasants side by side, and turn the birds in it until golden on all sides. Meantime, in another saucepan, melt a knob of butter and turn in it the apples, peeled and cored and quartered, until all the slices are well buttered. Arrange the pheasants breasts upwards, and pack them around with the apple pieces. Season lightly with salt and pepper, cover, and put in a moderate oven (190°C or 375°F, gas mark 5) for 40–50 minutes. Remove, whisk cream and Calvados together and stir gently into the apple mixture. Add more salt and pepper to taste and return to the oven to heat, uncovered, for five minutes. Serve directly from the pan without being too fussy about traditional carving methods.

Boeuf Bouilli à la Crème

A surprisingly quick and elegant way of dressing up left-over beef.

Ingredients

600–700 gr cooked beef (roast or casseroled), cut into thin slices

300 gr mushrooms (well-drained tinned ones do very well)

4 shallots

a good knob of butter

tablespoonful flour

1 dl cider

1 dl well-flavoured stock, or bouillon

2 dl cream

salt

freshly ground black pepper

lemon

Method

Arrange meat slices in a buttered oven dish, sprinkle with some of the cider and stock, cover with foil and put in a low oven to warm without cooking. Chop shallots finely and soften in melted butter, add the sliced mushrooms and a few drops of lemon juice. When the shallots are soft, stir in the flour and cook for a few minutes, and then add the rest of the cider and stock. Stir and cook until thick, season to taste, and pour over the meat. Return to the oven for a few minutes (or longer, if convenient) to allow the flavours to blend and then top with the cream. Warm in the oven for a few minutes longer before serving.

Omelette Normande

Ingredients

8 eggs
5 or 6 cooking apples
sugar to taste
pinch of salt

butter
1 wineglass Calvados
4 tablespoons cream

Method

Peel and slice the apples thinly and put in a covered shallow pan to soften with the melted butter, a little sugar, and a table-spoonful of Calvados. When barely tender, stir, sprinkle with a little more sugar and put in a moderate oven until sugar begins to caramelise. Meanwhile whisk eggs, cream, salt and another tablespoonful of Calvados and make the omelette in a hot pan with the rest of the butter. When set, slide on to a hot dish, cover with the apple mixture, dust with sugar and flame with the rest of the Calvados.

PART II

Brittany

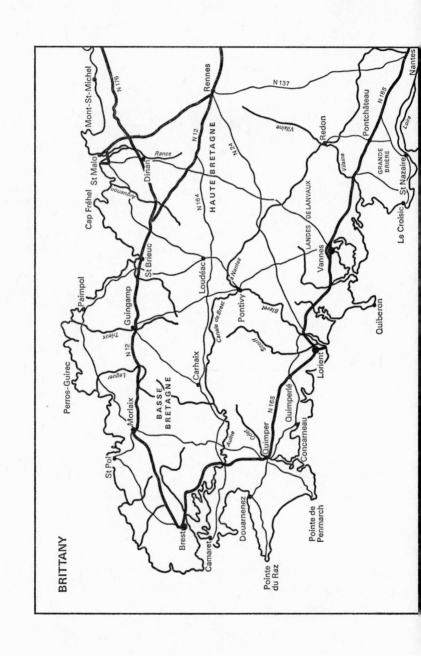

History

There is no frontier between Normandy and Brittany, but there is a definite sense of crossing some sort of barrier. In the north, it is represented by the Dol marshes, inland of Mont-St. Michel; in the south, by the marshes of the Grande Brière. There is even a perceptible change of topography, marked by the Rennes basin, entering central Brittany via Vitré.

In fact, Brittany's granite-based Armorican massif, caused by an upheaval of the earth's crust five hundred million years ago, extends well inland of its political border, so the geographical frontier is largely imaginary. But as one goes deeper into Brittany the granite becomes increasingly apparent. The central hills, worn down by millennia of erosion into a series of plateaux, are no longer high but they are scarred, with jagged outcrops, and the soil that covers them is thin. Where over the centuries men have felled the forests that partially covered these plateaux, wild heathland is now all that grows on them, and the granite protrudes like a skeleton beneath withered flesh.

Where the granite spills away on three sides to the sea, it becomes the framework of deep estuaries and craggy inlets, rising in fantastic rock shapes around and between them. And everywhere the granite is manifest in man's artefacts; in the sturdy ochre-grey or whitewashed stone farmhouses, and the village churches, and the fortresses, and the buildings in the towns and above all, in the strange rough monuments that existed thousands of years before any of them: the lines of standing-stones, or *alignements*, the lone menhirs, and the stone tombs or dolmens.

The granite has also played its part in shaping the Breton

people, certainly, making of them tough explorers and fishermen and tenacious smallholders, but no one knows anything of the people who shaped these megaliths. Whoever they were, they not only knew enough about mathematics to align their monuments with remarkable accuracy, but also knew how to mine their tin and copper and to trade both by land and sea. Whether they were driven away or absorbed by the Celts who arrived in the 6th century BC is still a mystery. But these Celtic tribes, who settled in five distinct areas (approximating, oddly enough, to the five administrative departments into which Brittany was divided after the Revolution) are the first peoples of whom any written evidence exists, thanks to the Romans who eventually conquered them. These first Gauls gave the name Armor, or land of the sea, to the coastal areas, and called their inland regions the Argoat, or land of the woods, and both suffixes still frequently appear on modern maps.

Of these five tribes the most powerful was the Veneti, the earliest Breton seafarers, who inhabited the Morbihan area around Vannes. When the Romans arrived in the 1st century BC, it was with them that the fiercest battle was fought, for Caesar saw them as a threat to his trade routes and destroyed their fleet outside the Morbihan Gulf in 56 BC. Thereafter Armorica, as it became known, remained a Roman province for some four centuries, wealthy at first and then slowly drained by heavy taxation until the Romans withdrew and left it to sink into savagery.

The first immigrants from Britain came in about AD 460 and continued to come for about two hundred years, mostly in groups under the leadership of monks who were subsequently unofficially elevated to sainthood and their names conferred upon a multitude of the villages and towns that grew out of their original settlements.

Thus a new language, new customs, a new religion and scores of new saints as well as the new name of Brittany came to Armorica and spurred its regeneration. With these new Bretons also came a mass of superstitions—beliefs in witches and wizards and fairies and demons—and a cobweb of legends in which Christianity and paganism were inextricably mixed. The tales of the Holy Grail are as much part of Breton folklore as of English, for some versions have it that Joseph of Arimathea landed in Brittany rather than Britain with the sacred Cup. Merlin and the fairy Viviane are also bound up in Breton lore; so are Tristram and Iseult; so especially is the story of the submerged city of Ys.

Returning to recorded history, Charlemagne conquered Brittany in 799, but the allegiance to Frankish rule of such a fey and basically Celtic people, and one so traditionally parochial, was remote. Charlemagne accordingly delegated some authority to a local noble, one Nominoë, creating him Count of Vannes. Twenty-seven years later, Charlemagne's last remaining son, Louis, raised Nominoë to the rank of Duke. But Nominoë had more serious ambitions and, on Louis's death he rallied his Bretons and defeated Charles the Bald at Redon in 843, whereupon he had himself crowned King of an independent Brittany at Dol.

The kingdom started to crumble, however, following the death of his nephew Salomon in 874, and successive Norman invasions hastened the process. For nearly half a century chaos reigned until another Vannois nobleman, Count Alain, launched a campaign to expel the Normans. This was successfully concluded by his godson, Duke Alain Barbe-Torte, at Questambert in 939, but for unexplained reasons Duke Alain did not reward himself with a crown. Even so, the peace he had brought about was short-lived, and on his death in 952 the feudal lords, whose castles he had strengthened to repel the Normans, set about defying both his heirs and one another. Brittany once again became divided and the Dukes of Vannes had little control over them. When William the Conqueror became King of England matters did not improve: Brittany was manoeuvred into being a sort of buffer state between England and Normandy, with the Dukes vainly trying to hold the balance of power.

Eventually, a weak and weary Duke called Conan IV enlisted the aid of Henry II of England against his vassals and, in desperation, ceded the throne to Henry in 1166. Conan's daughter Constance married Henry's son Geoffrey Plantagenet, but their son, Arthur, was murdered—by King John of England, in 1203, to prevent him from being a threat to the English throne. Thus Arthur's half-sister, Alice, and her French husband Pierre of Dreux, succeeded to the Duchy, founding a new line of Dukes who at least had the advantage of French support and consequently managed to maintain a modicum of authority for over a century.

But in 1341, the death of Duke Jean III unleashed yet another power struggle, the War of Succession, which was to become the bloodiest of them all. The official contenders were Duke Jean's heir apparent, Charles of Blois, who had married the Duke's niece Jeanne de Penthièvre, and Jeanne's brother, Jean de Montfort, whose wife, to complicate matters, was also called Jeanne (of Flanders). It might have been a purely local conflict had not the French King, Philippe IV, entered the lists in support of Charles of Blois, his nephew, while Edward III of England took the side of Jean de Montfort.

(This war begat one of the greatest soldiers in French history, incidentally: Bertrand du Guesclin, a Breton whose name crops up again and again during the Hundred Years War and is associated with more than a dozen decisive battles. Born in about 1320 near Dinan, at the heart of the region that was loyal to Charles of Blois and his Jeanne, he naturally entered their ranks in the War of Succession. When this struggle ended, after more than twenty years, in a decisive victory for Jean de Montfort at the Battle of Auray in 1364, in which Charles of

Blois was killed, du Guesclin was taken prisoner. But he was shortly released and went to serve the King of France, turning his military skill for the next fifteen years against the English and gradually driving them out of much of Aquitaine.)

The end of the War of Succession found Brittany in a sad state. A new young Duke, Jean IV, returned from exile in England to succeed the elder de Montfort and to try to restore order and prosperity to the shattered dukedom. Despite a series of clashes with one Olivier de Clisson, a fanatical supporter first of the English and then, after 1370, of the French, Jean IV and his successors managed to pull their country together and the following century was one of the most brilliant in its history. It was not entirely peaceful though; although the Dukes were sovereigns in all but name, they had to fight almost continuously to keep their authority. One of the most notable of these warrior Dukes was Arthur III, Constable de Richemont, who ruled from 1451 for seven years; just before succeeding, he had united with the French King to drive the English from France and thus end the Hundred Years War.

The last notable Montfort Duke was François II—he who kept the English Henry of Lancaster (Henry Tudor, who became Henry VII in 1485) and his uncle prisoners for nearly fourteen years after they had fled to Brittany during the Wars of the Roses. An ardent champion of Breton independence and in constant rebellion against the French crown, François II fought his final battle at St. Aubin-du-Cormier, between Rennes and Fougères, and lost. He died shortly afterwards, of grief it is said, and was succeeded by his daughter Anne, then aged eleven, in 1488.

La Duchesse Anne, Anne of Brittany, 'la petite Brette'—one constantly meets one or another of her names throughout the country, for she is the best-remembered of all the Breton rulers. Her portraits show her as chubby and cheerful rather than beautiful, but she seems to have made up in character, intelligence and charm for whatever she lacked in looks and her Duchy was an irresistible attraction. Despite having been married by proxy at thirteen to the future Emperor of Austria, she was courted by Charles VIII of France (himself also theoretically bound, in an unconsummated union, to an Austrian princess). In 1491 Charles pressed his suit by besieging Rennes and Anne agreed to meet him. They liked one another; although Charles's face was far from handsome, there are signs of humour and even sensitivity in his portraits. At all events, after obtaining Papal agreement to the dissolution of their previous marriages, they celebrated their own at the end of that year and seem to have suited one another admirably.

Seven years later, the King died and Anne returned to Brittany, which had remained an independent Duchy. In a year's time she was again married to a French King, Louis XII. But she had no sons, and when she died in 1514 at the age of thirty-seven the Duchy passed to her eldest daughter, Claude, who brought Brittany to France as part of her dowry when she married the future François I, formally ceding it to the crown on her early death in 1532. Their son was Henri II, who succeeded in 1547 to a kingdom that for the first time included the Breton peninsula.

Brittany, however, retained a partially independent parliament whose authority was based on the terms of Anne's marriage contract with Louis XII, which stipulated a measure of respect for the ancient customs of the Duchy; and revolts against too heavy-handed French rule were frequent. It was not only Bretons who sought autonomy for their province, either: in 1588 the Governor, the Duke of Mercoeur, a strong Catholic supporter, plotted to take it over himself during the Wars of Religion and the people revolted, eventually seeking the help of Henri IV of France in 1598. The result was the Edict of Nantes, which ushered in religious toleration and temporarily brought peace to Brittany once more.

But excessive taxation under Louis XIV's minister, Colbert, caused another Breton revolt in 1675, and again nearly a hundred years later the Breton parliament, in its determination to weaken the power of the Jesuits, revolted against the absolute power of the crown and gained the support of the parliament in Paris for their cause. This was in 1764, just quarter of a century before the French Revolution, at first heartily welcomed in Brittany as the end of royal autocracy, but later opposed thanks to the laws passed against the Church and its priests and to the taxes imposed by the Republican government. By 1794 a Breton royalist faction (the Chouans) were in revolt, but when a royalist force under the protection of the English fleet attempted to land at Carnac in 1795, it was trounced and Chouan resistance crumbled thereafter and, despite a couple of attempts to revive the cause in the 19th century (notably by the Duchesse de Berry in 1832), eventually died. Brittany's political fusion with France was complete but the people, staunchly Catholic and resentful of their Republican rulers' secularity, resisted the idea of identifying themselves with the French as a whole until forced to do so by the advent of war.

The First World War left Brittany virtually unscathed but during the second conflict Brest, Lorient and St. Nazaire became German naval bases, and the majority of Bretons allied themselves with the F.F.I. (Forces Françaises de l'Intérieur). The province was almost entirely liberated in under a fortnight in August 1944, following General Patton's lightning advance south from Avranches; only Brest, Lorient, Quiberon and St. Nazaire held out—and suffered great damage.

Breton art and architecture does not emerge in any recognisable form until the early 15th century. The ancient megaliths of prehistoric times were converted to serve the early Gauls, the Romans, and the Celtic colonists from Britain alike, by means of crude carvings which adapted them to the needs of each successive religion. During the 10th and 11th centuries when Romanesque art was flourishing in Normandy and the more southerly provinces, Brittany was both too poor and too war-torn to indulge in the luxury of building churches. Granite is, in any case, a difficult stone to work; consequently, when comparative peace came to Brittany under the Montfort Dukes, Gothic art was in flower, and Breton religious architecture is an adaptation of this style: simpler in many respects, thanks to the hardness of the stone, more ornate in others where wood was used instead.

Cathedrals and big churches are few: less than thirty in all. More characteristic are the hundreds of small churches and tiny chapels, many with intricately carved wooden rood beams and screens. Unique, though, are Brittany's carved stone Calvaries, or crucifixions: freestanding monuments, varying in size and wealth of detail and normally situated in churchyards. Nearby there is often an ossuary, and an elaborate archway leading to the cemetery, and these three elements, together with the church itself, make up the typical 'parish close'.

The great granite fortresses that guard the borders of Brittany are the earliest examples of domestic architecture to be seen—if indeed these massive edifices can be counted as domestic. But granite was also used in many of the old houses, whose lower storeys are often of stone, supporting half-timbered upper parts whose external beams are often beautifully carved. Elaborately worked wood is also a feature of domestic furniture, particularly the enclosed beds and the huge chests, of which the best examples are to be seen in the regional museums.

Brittany has produced more soldiers than artists, but has bred its fair share of scholars and writers. Among the earliest was the 12th-century Pierre Abélard, the brilliant ecclesiastical teacher, remembered more nowadays for his love of Héloise;

the historian Guillaume Le Breton in the 13th century; and the biographer of Breton saints, Albert Legrand, in the 15th. The indefatigable 17th-century letter-writer, Madame de Sévigné, was a Breton by marriage; Lesage, 18th-century author of *Gil Blas*, was a native of Vannes. In more recent times the best-known names are those of Chateaubriand and Lamennais, both writers of national stature; also Jules Verne (a Nantais) and Pierre Loti.

None of these, with the possible exception of Loti and Legrand, conveyed a great deal of the Breton character in their writings, although Chateaubriand's imaginative powers and intensity owe much to his background. But the Breton character is an elusive one to define. A mystical streak pervades Breton faith, finding its most dramatic expression in the many 'pardons', or annual Saints' day festivals, held throughout the province. At the same time the Breton is deeply superstitious, with a Celtic melancholy and sense of poetry, and a vivid imagination often concealed by apparent taciturnity. In any case, there are two sorts of Breton: those from Haute Bretagne, to the east of a line running roughly south from St. Brieuc through Pontivy to Carnac, who for centuries have been more French than Celt; and those of the west, or Basse Bretagne, who keep their ancient dialect and customs more jealously intact and sometimes appear to have more in common with the Welsh or the Irish than with their Haute Bretagne compatriots. It is in this part of the country that the vast majority of the more important 'pardons' are held, and where one is most likely to see the traditional costumes and *coiffes* (starched lace and linen head-dresses), for though the demarcation line between Haute and Basse Bretagne has become blurred in modern times, a strong movement to revive and preserve regional customs, folklore and language has recently been launched and may well counteract the erosion of the Breton character.

Specialities

As might be expected of a people who were more concerned to build churches than castles, the excellence of Breton cuisine owed more to nature than to art in the past: the paramount characteristic being the marvellous variety and freshness of the sea-food, and of the fruits and vegetables grown in the sheltered, temperate valleys, and the distinctive flavour of the sheep raised on the salt marshes. None of these qualities has altered, but the spread of civilisation has resulted in a more sophisticated attitude towards the preparation of food, which now begins to hold its own with other, more renowned regional gastronomy. As in Normandy, the local drink is cider, but except for the variety grown in the extreme south-west it is not of prime quality. On the other hand, Brittany can boast its excellent Muscadet wines from the Loire valley around Nantes, and the two rougher wines of Gros Plant and Rhuys.

One does not, therefore, need to sacrifice gastronomic pleasure to enjoy exploring Brittany: far from it. The fact that so many of its most delectable foods are either difficult or prohibitively expensive to come by elsewhere is reason enough to embark upon an unrepeatable gastronomic whirl the moment one crosses the border, chasing such delicacies as lobster (*homard grillé*, or *à l'armoricaine*, sometimes mis-spelt as *l'américaine*) and stuffed clams and mussels (*palourdes* or *moules farcies*), and rich *feuilleté* pastry filled with shrimps and mussels and crayfish, and all sorts of sea-fish garnished with the incomparable *beurre blanc* sauce. Bretons have wonderful ways with vegetables, too, especially in soups: their turnips, for instance, seem to bear no relation to turnips from anywhere else. And it is a grave mistake to equate *crêperies* purely with cheap take-away food, because the variety of pancake-fillings, both savoury and sweet, to be sampled in the good ones is a revelation; one could lunch off *crêpes* for weeks without duplicating flavours.

The far greater problem is how best to plan one's exploration without duplication, for so much of the coast is so jagged that to be based by the sea means wasting a lot of time and energy retracing tracks; unless one *must* be on a beach for the sake of the children, it is probably better to stay slightly inland at a point from which one can radiate in several directions. The sea, in any case, is seldom very far away.

Haute Bretagne: The North

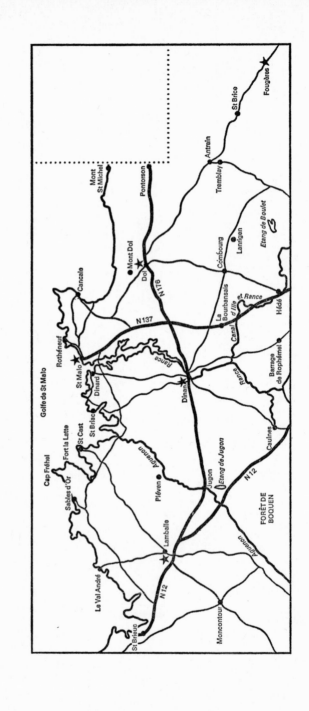

Dividing Brittany purely arbitrarily, with no regard for departmental frontiers, I have chosen to start with the northern part of Haute Bretagne, because it leads on easily from Normandy. One reaches it by one of two ways. The first is from Mont-St. Michel to Dol across the reclaimed salt marshes and polders, occasionally bisected by rows of close-cropped trees that have been overgrown with ivy and thus look like rows of waifs wrapped in rags. They are a strange sight in a strange-looking landscape—cross it here, and one can see very easily how Mont-St. Michel could again become part of the mainland by the end of the century through continuous silting up of the bay.

The alternative route to Dol is more roundabout, from the oddly laid out shoe-manufacturing town of **Fougères** to the south, with its centre above and to the east of its colossal castle. The most famous baron of this heavily restored, former frontier fortress was one Raoul II, who defied the decision of Duke Conan IV to abdicate in favour of England's Henry II in 1166 and paid for it by having his castle razed. Undeterred, he rebuilt it, and the complex still contains parts of his reconstruction as well as 13th- and 14th-century additions by the next owners, the Lusignans from Poitou, and others later still. Once it was entirely moated by the Nançon river, in whose valley it stands, but the outer loop is now filled in. Walking around the outside as well as the inside, skirting neat little kitchen gardens sheltering beneath its walls, one gets a splendid impression of how vast a stronghold it was in mediaeval times.

In the flamboyant Gothic church of St. Sulpice, alongside it, is an unusual 12th-century statue, Notre-Dame-des-Marais, suckling her infant, and past this church, around the Place du

Marchix, are the most interesting parts of the town's oldest quarter. A bridge across the river links it with the Escalier de la Duchesse Anne, leading up the side of the valley to the sheer ramparts overhead. Gardens have been terraced out of the slopes below them, ending in the Place aux Arbres – which, in fact, is probably the best starting point for a tour of Fougères because its superb views provide splendid orientation. But, whichever way round one goes, one should plan to arrive at the third point of this triangle, Place Gambetta, in time for lunch at the *Restaurant des Voyageurs*. It will make all the walking worthwhile, and the hotel of the same name makes an agreeable overnight stop.

By branching left off the main road from Fougères to Antrain some 6 kilometres (4 miles) after St. Brice-en-Coglès, it is possible to pass through Tremblay, with one of Brittany's few Romanesque churches, and then wind into Antrain via the handsome castle of Bonne-Fontaine (gardens open on Sundays). It is then tempting not to go straight on to Dol but instead detour westwards to **Combourg**, true castle-fanatics perhaps making a slight extra detour to pass the enchanting little Château de Lanrigan to the south-east of it. That has the added advantage of bringing one into Combourg at the opposite end from the power station, skirting a small lake and arriving at the western and most attractive part of this old granite town, beneath the castle walls. The castle's interest lies not in the fact that it dates back to the 11th century, when it belonged to the du Guesclins, but in its associations with Chateaubriand, whose father bought it, and anyone who has read his memoirs will want to look it over briefly. The two years he spent here as a child must certainly have been dull and lonely, but to see the castle and his room today is to realise what drama a vivid imagination can conjure up from fairly prosaic material.

Midway between Combourg and Dol, using minor roads, is

the Château de Landal, a Renaissance building with impressive ramparts in a lovely setting of trees and lakelets, well worth a look (the interior is not open but the courtyard and ramparts are), and then one is within 13 kilometres (8 miles) of the quaint little marooned city of **Dol-de-Bretagne**.

Dol looks marooned because it sits on the edge of a low cliff that was until some twelve hundred years ago lapped by the sea, which then extended up to 10 kilometres (over 6 miles) further inland than at present, almost cutting off the St. Malo peninsula altogether. Consequently Dol has a slightly abandoned air, as though still mourning both the departed waves and its vanished glories, for it was an important bishopric in the Middle Ages. Nominoë of Vannes was crowned King in the first cathedral to stand here, which King John of England burned in 1203, and the present 13th–14th-century Norman Gothic building seems vast in relation to the town itself. The west front is dull, but much of the rest of it is very beautiful, particularly the great south porch, and the unfinished north tower. From the tree-lined promenade behind the old cathedral are wonderful views across the alluvial plain with the distinctive hump of Mont-Dol in the foreground; this ancient mound, where the remains of mammoths and other prehistoric beasts have been unearthed, was an island for centuries, and before that a hilltop protruding from woodlands. Legend has it that St. Michael fought a duel with the Devil here and the devout can trace the marks supposedly made by Satan's claws as he fell, and by the archangel's foot as he bounded away to Mont-St. Michel.

Dol is a pleasant place in which to spend a night or two (one could easily visit Mont-St. Michel from here) for it is quiet and there is a choice of good small hotels: the *Bretagne*, which is simpler, and the *Logis Bresche Arthur*, slightly grander. It makes a good starting point for the St. Malo peninsula, too. Going anti-clockwise, one crosses acres of reclaimed land before coming to **Cancale**, of oyster fame, where a fisherman's daughter named Jeanne Jugon was born in 1792. She became a maidservant in St. Servan (now a suburb of St. Malo) and, with the 400 francs her mistress left her when she died, founded the order of Little Sisters of the Poor.

Her birthplace is just inland of Cancale, on the direct road to St. Malo, but it is more scenic even on a dull day to follow the coast instead, dribbling away into rocky islets. There are fine beaches at La Guimorais and, to the west of it, the tightly enclosed bay of Rothéneuf is sheltered enough for water sports at high tide and almost empty when the sea recedes. Paramé, on the northern outskirts of St. Malo, is a sprawling resort and spa; the main road leads straight through it and across the causeway between port and sea to the magnificent St. Vincent gateway, beneath the castle walls, and into the heart of St. Malo itself.

St. Malo Intra-Muros (within the walls) is another ferry port for services to England and deservedly one of the chief tourist sights of Brittany, not least because of the amazingly faithful way it has been reconstructed after the almost complete devastation of 1944. There is no visible evidence today that it even suffered any such damage, but a visit to the Musée d'Histoire and its exhibition of wartime photographs punches the reality home and leaves one full of awe and admiration. The museum also contains relics of St. Malo's more famous sons. Jacques Cartier was one: he sailed in search of gold in Newfoundland and Labrador in 1535 but instead found himself navigating the St. Lawrence river.

Other seafaring *malouins* were the 'legalised' privateers, best-known of whom were Duguay-Trouin who started as a cabin boy and ended as a titled and high-ranking naval officer, and Surcouf, who had made enough to retire upon at the age of thirty-six; these two and many others, whose operations were licensed by the Crown, amassed fortunes while bedevilling the ships of their country's enemies. The story of another St. Malo seafarer of almost unbelievable integrity is also remembered here: the 17th-century Porcon de la Barbinais, who was retained by the local shipowners to protect their ships against the Barbary pirates and instead was captured by them. The Bey of Algiers released him to negotiate a truce with Louis XIV, on condition that he should return if he failed. He did fail and, having dallied only long enough to bid farewell to his family, he did return—to execution.

The Musée d'Histoire also contains portraits of Chateaubriand, who was born here and who is buried on the Grand Bé islet due west of the town, and of the priest-philosopher Lamennais, son of another St. Malo shipowner, who spent much of his life both here and at the Château de la Chesnaie, between Combourg and Dinan.

From an unprepossessing opening in the town walls between the museum and the St. Vincent gateway, a flight of steps climbs to the top of the ramparts and the broad pathway along the top. It is a fascinating walk, with views outward across the port, the Rance estuary and the sea, and inwards across the chimneys and rooftops of former shipowners' mansions, a few of them original, others reconstructions, but most—to judge by the forests of television aerials—now subdivided into apartments. Bastions and towers break the lines of the walls, and there are statues of *malouin* seamen gazing like stout Cortez, with eagle eyes, out to the oceans they conquered. At the steps just before the Bidouane Tower I like to come down into the town again and walk through it: there is always plenty of life, even out of season, thanks to the presence of merchant navy trainees, and lots of good shops and cafés, and the restoration of the former Cathedral of St. Vincent has been beautifully done. There are good fish restaurants both within and without the walled part of the city, particularly *Duchesse Anne*, built almost into the ramparts, and a nice little hotel near the central market place (the *Noguette*) where one wakes in the morning to the raucous cries of the vendors.

Twisting south alongside the numerous and always crowded basins of the port, St. Malo shades without interruption into St. Servan, in itself not very interesting. The **Aleth** promontory at its tip, though, was the site of the original Gallo-Roman settlement in the Rance estuary: it was here that St. Malo himself arrived from Wales in the 6th century. Not until the mid-12th century was the site abandoned for the present one to the north of it. The walk around Aleth is as interesting as the one round St. Malo, starting alongside the ruins of the former cathedral, skirting the harbour, passing the City Fort (built in 1759, greatly strengthened by the Germans in the Second World War, and now containing an open-air theatre), and returning along the westernmost corniche towards the two little ports to the south which are separated by the Tour Solidor. Consisting of three towers, pressed together like the pipes of Pan, and rising from Roman foundations, the Tour Solidor was built at the end of the Breton War of Succession by the victorious young de Montfort Duke, Jean IV, as a counter-stronghold to that of the intransigent *malouins*; later it was used as a prison and it now houses a museum of Cape Horn ships.

Aleth makes a pleasant detour from the main road between St. Malo and Dinard, which runs along the top of the tidal dam across the Rance estuary, and **Dinard** is certainly a more popular (and more expensive) staging-post on a tour of this part of Brittany than is St. Malo. Prim, pretty and immaculately kept, with its three sweeping beaches and its Casino and its smart shops and tidy villas, it was 'discovered' and colonised by Americans in the mid-19th century and developed, both by them and by the British who followed them, into an international resort. The smaller resorts to the west like St. Lunaire, St. Briac and Lancieux are quieter and less sophisticated.

An excellent reason for lingering either in Dinard or St. Malo is to take a boat trip up the Rance to **Dinan**; one can equally well do it in the other direction, of course, but schedules are more likely to be devised for the convenience of the coast-based tourist. It is also somehow more impressive to start at the seaward end, chugging up towards the great electricity generating station beside the dam and entering the lock; rising majestically with the water level and then drifting out through the southern gate on to the smooth surface of what is now, in effect, a lake. The high banks to either side sometimes form narrow straits and in other places retreat into the distance, framing wide expanses of water; above them are farms and villages and lovely mansions built as country retreats by the rich shipowners of St. Malo. The last wide stretch is upstream of the St. Hubert bridge; after Mordreuc, one of the few villages actually at the water's edge, the course of the river narrows until it is scarcely wider than a canal on the final approach to Dinan.

In an ideal world, one would disembark at Dinan and not return down the Rance at all—though it looks quite different going in the other direction. One's car, if one were travelling by road, would be driven inland by someone else and would be waiting in the Place du Champ-Clos, outside the *Hôtel d'Avaugour* which, although close to a sometimes noisy main thoroughfare, is perfectly charming, with delicious food, and makes a splendid base for a few days.

However one gets to Dinan, though, one needs several days there, for it is a gem of a place. The Place du Champ-Clos is the spot on which in 1359, during a siege by English troops under the Duke of Lancaster, Bertrand du Guesclin defeated an English knight in single combat. It is hard to imagine this duel, which was fought because the English had violated a truce and captured du Guesclin's brother, taking place on what is now a thoroughly civilised square, shaded with pollarded trees and full of parked cars.

But in other parts of the old city of Dinan one is instantly transported backwards through the centuries: in the Place des Cordeliers and the Place des Merciers, in rue du Jerzual, rue de la Lainerie, rue de l'Apport and rue Croix-Quart. Old houses with triangular gables rest their timber-framed upper storeys, each projecting a little further than the one beneath it, on pillars of granite or wood, forming arcades over the pavements; there are stone-mullioned windows and stone doorways and oddly placed turrets; there are tiny alleyways and courtyards and fine mansions; there is the strange 15th-century clock tower in the picturesque rue de l'Horloge. The basilica of St. Sauveur has a lopsided look to it, its south side pure Romanesque while the north side is flamboyant Gothic. Beneath a 15th-century memorial in the north arm of the transept, du Guesclin's heart is buried at his own request, for he was born near Dinan and married a Dinan girl soon after the episode in the Place du Champ-Clos. (His body is in Paris at St. Denis, and his wife's tomb is in the Prieuré de Lehon, further up the Rance, her effigy dressed in warrior's armour.)

Behind St. Sauveur, the former churchyard is now laid out as a garden, full of shrubs and reaching as far as the city ramparts. Mimosa, japonica and forsythia start blooming there as early as February, and it has a beautiful view down to the Rance, studded with pleasure boats and crossed by a (reconstructed) granite bridge in the Gothic style.

Coming back to the western part of Dinan (one can follow the line of the ramparts, which date from the 13th and 14th centuries, almost all the way round the town), the huge Place du Guesclin flanks the Place du Champ-Clos, with the old warrior's statue at one end. At the other end rises the wonderful mediaeval castle, parts of which can be visited, including the Tour de Coëtquen and the Donjon de la Duchesse Anne, which contains the town museum.

The country around Dinan is a joy, too, with the great forests of Coëtquen and Le Mesnil to the east, and the splendid Château de la Bourbonsais near **Pleuguenec** to the south of them, which has flocks of birds and other wildlife in its grounds and a beautiful, formal garden full of elaborately shaped flowerbeds and pathways and stone urns. From here minor roads southwards criss-cross the Canal d'Ille et Rance as far as **Hédé**, whose ruined castle rides a rocky ridge to which old houses and gardens cling. West of this, along a pretty little road, is the Château de Montmuran, its huge gateway dwarfed by enormous round towers and reached by a drawbridge across a moat; the original building was razed by Henry II of England in 1168, and the present one dates from the following century. It was here that du Guesclin was knighted. It stands just outside the hamlet of **Les Iffs** with a charming Gothic church containing some good stained glass. A little further west again, still following minor roads, is the formally proportioned Château de Caradeuc, once the home of the 18th-century Breton parliamentary rebel, La Chalotais.

Westwards again, the road runs along a ridge, past a ruined prehistoric *alignement*, with views across the twin-pronged Rophémel dam to the north, and into Caulnes, passing the beautifully balanced outlines of the Château of Couëlan on the way; from here Dinan is a bare 24 kilometres (16 miles).

Dinan is an equally good centre for exploring even further west. Jutting out into the mussel-rich bay between St. Lunaire and St. Cast is a little promontory with the old village of St. Jacut spilling over it down to a series of little beaches separated by rocks, with the Hébihen islets, covered in seabirds, trailing away from it. **St. Cast** itself is a scattered resort with two long beaches where English children's voices can be heard in the summer holiday season; some two hundred years ago it must have reverberated with less happy noises when an English force, in retreat after an abortive attack on

St. Malo, was thoroughly trounced.

Across the wedge-shaped Baie de la Frenaye to the west of St. Cast is one of the most impressive of Breton fortresses: Fort la Latte, rising from a rocky mound that appears to have partly broken away from the mainland and is thus almost surrounded by the sea. Dating back to mediaeval times, though rebuilt in the late 17th century, it has a marvellous air of feudal aloofness. It has marvellous views, too, though not as spectacular as those from Cap Fréhel, an amazing mixture of red, grey and black cliff-faces that in certain lights look almost purple; to drive down from Cap Fréhel to Sables d'Or towards sunset is a dramatic experience.

Inland, between the Forest of Hunaudaie and the long, narrow reservoir created by the damming of the Arguenon, stands the ruined Château de la Hunaudaie, originally built in the 13th century, damaged during the War of Succession, rebuilt and enlarged in the late 14th and early 15th centuries and partly demolished during the Revolution—an immensely evocative remnant of stormy centuries. Nearby, a 15th-century manor house at Pléven has been transformed into a luxury hotel in a park that is near enough to the reservoir for some lovely walks.

The reservoir narrows to river-width at Jugon and widens again to the south of it into the Etang de Jugon, a popular fishing spot. Going back to Dinan from here one could go through **Corseulles**, where enough remains have been found to suggest that it was the headquarters of one of the original Gaulish tribes in Brittany; just beyond the village up a little lane is a ruined octagonal tower known locally as the Temple of Mars which is certainly of Gallo-Roman construction.

At Jugon, though, one is more than halfway between Dinan and **Lamballe**, a pleasant little market town with the nice *Hôtel d'Angleterre* near the railway station (ask for a room at the rear) which is very adequate for an overnight stop en route westwards. Part of the French National Stud is housed at Lamballe, and within walking distance of it is the church of Notre-Dame, formerly the chapel of the now ruined castle, looking down across the Gouessant valley. The little town's name is best remembered, however, for its unfortunate young Princesse de Lamballe, lady-in-waiting to Marie Antoinette, whose head was bloodily severed by a revolutionary mob in 1792.

Southwards of Lamballe, surrounded by the Boquen forest, is the Cistercian Abbaye de Boquen, founded in the 12th century and abandoned in the Revolution, but now re-inhabited and partly restored; it was the burial place of Gilles de Bretagne, handed over to murderers by his brother, Duke François I, in 1450, for having conspired with the English. Heading west, towards Moncontour, the solitary castle of Touche-Trébry lies just beyond the village of Trébry; it looks mediaeval but was in fact built at the end of the 16th century. Quite close to it is the famous chapel of Notre-Dame-du-Haut where are the six wooden statues of Brittany's healer saints: St. Livertin, clasping his temples, who with Ste. Eugénie heals headaches; St. Mamertin, curer of colic; St. Léobin, who relieves rheumatism; St. Méen, healer of sick minds; St. Hubert, who deals with sores and rabies; and Ste. Houarniaule, calmer of nervous fears. The chapel is often locked, but the key is kept at the nearby farm.

Moncontour is a charming little fortified town on a precipitous spur above the junction of two valleys. At its heart is an elegant 18th-century square, on one side of which the church of St. Mathurin rejoices in six exceptional 16th-century windows. Just south of the town is Bel-Air, one of the highest eminences in this part of Brittany; to the north is the pleasant but unexciting town of St. Brieuc.

Haute Bretagne: The Interior

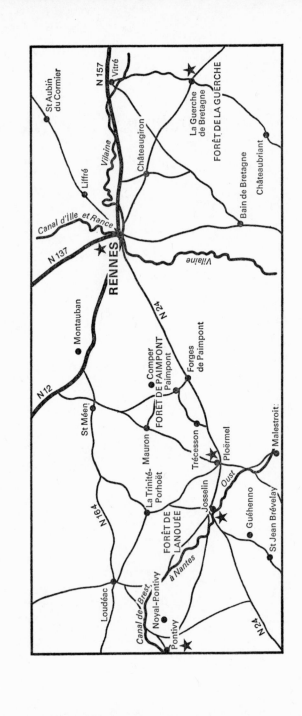

This is a region most people rush through en route to some-where else, crossing it diagonally from north-east to south-west or vice versa, vaguely thinking that parts of it look rather attractive and worth investigating one day, but forever putting that day off. I have done it myself, pushing on after Fougères and hoping to get past Rennes before the evening rush hour, missing the bits between several times. Actually, it is a lovely pastoral region and pleasantly empty except for trees, as one discovers if one stops to picnic, for the Forests of St. Aubin, Liffré, Chevré and of Rennes itself are remnants of the wood-lands that once clothed much of Brittany, all spangled with lakes and streams. Near St. Aubin-du-Cormier is a plaque commemorating the battle of 1488 in which Duke François II, father of Anne of Brittany, lost his country's independence to France.

Even more interesting are the approaches to Rennes via Vitré or Châteaubriant. Just south of Vitré, cloaked in wood-lands, is the Château of Les Rochers where that indefatigable letter-writer, Madame de Sévigné, spent a great deal of her life, chronicling with as much wit and verve the dullish life she led there (partly for economy's sake) as she applied to her tales of Versailles and the court of Louis XIV. Her room in the castle, and its grounds, can be visited. **Vitré** itself is one of the best-preserved old towns in Brittany, a secretive tangle of old streets hugged inside ramparts, best seen from the north, alongside the Fougères road. Its walls rear up above the Vilaine and culminate in the golden-brown castle, riding the westernmost point of the ridge like the prow of a ship. It has been faithfully restored more or less to its original 14th- and 15th-century form, and contains a small museum. Within the old part of the town, to the east of the castle, Notre-Dame church dates from the 15th century and has an oddly gabled south side with an external pulpit from which preachers used to harangue the Calvinists; Vitré was staunchly Protestant, for which it incurred the scorn of Madame de Sévigné. Some lovely old houses are still to be seen there, recalling the provincial *beau monde* which Madame de Sévigné also mocked, their upper storeys projecting over the pavements and supported on carved pillars.

A few miles to the north-west of the town is an exceptionally pretty village: **Champeaux**, with a harmonious central square that looks like a picture-postcard. To the south of it, **La Guerche-de-Bretagne** has some vivid Gothic misericords in a church that is otherwise disappointing and another equally pleasant surprise in the form of a small hotel, the *Pinault*, that does miraculous meals for paltry sums. One can work up an appetite—or work off the excesses—by circling to the west of the little town and walking at least part of the way from the shores of the Marcillé lake to the Roche-aux-Fées, an extraordinary megalithic structure, one of the biggest in Brittany, consisting of a covered corridor and a large stone chamber. No one knows exactly what its original purpose was; it is not thought to be a dolmen, and it is enveloped in legend and superstition.

South again, another approach to Rennes is through **Châteaubriant**, from whose counts—despite the differences in the spelling—the writer François-René de Chateaubriand claimed descent. The château, which covers a large area and is in two sections, sits in the centre of town, its Renaissance buildings facing the remains of the feudal castle and now occupied by the law courts. One can visit the rooms where for ten years a young countess was supposedly imprisoned by her jealous husband, enraged because she had briefly been the mistress of France's King François I, yet grimly building the new château for her up to the moment when he is said to have murdered her.

From Châteaubriant, from La Guerche, from Vitré and, indeed, from all the eastern approaches to Brittany, all the main roads converge upon the capital, **Rennes**. It is a prosperous city, with its factories and its agricultural trades; it is also a lively city, with its university generating a constant stream of young people through its streets and boulevards. It is a historic city, too, descended from the tribal headquarters of the Gaulish Redones, and although it was largely destroyed by fire in 1720 it is also a handsome city, having been rebuilt on harmonious Classical lines conceived by the architect Jacques Gabriel, father of the designer of the Place de la Concorde in Paris. It is obviously a place for the serious traveller to stay in for a while, and this I confess I have never done. I can vouch for the excellence of the Breton museum, which has a beautifully displayed collection of costumes and artefacts, and I have walked the old streets around the cathedral, where some typical overhanging Breton mansions remain—including the restaurant *Ti-Koz* in the rue St. Guillaume which is said to have been the house of du Guesclin. But nowhere have I been able to capture the Breton spirit of Rennes—the place where du Guesclin as a young and by no means handsome man first fought his way into the limelight in a local tournament; the place where little Anne of Brittany accepted the hand of her first French king; the place where the provincial parliament, led by La Chalotais, was the first popular body to defy the absolute power of the monarch over the matter of the Jesuits in 1764. All that was truly Breton in Rennes has seemingly been burned away and the correct town of today fails to recall it.

In total contrast, the essence of ancient Brittany is so strongly present that it is almost tangible in the environs of Paimpont, just 24 kilometres (16 miles) west of Rennes. Coming to it along minor roads, through Montfort and Iffendic, rather than burning along the main N24, the atmosphere makes itself felt stealthily as one enters the ancient forest of Brociélande, setting of some of the earliest romances of chivalry. Here is the castle of Comper, where the fairy Viviane is said to have been born; here is the Baranton fountain where the wizard Merlin, having left King Arthur's court, fell under Viviane's spell; here is the Val sans Retour where the witch Morgane (Morgan the Fay) lured untrue knights to nameless punishments. Although the western part of the forest is now used for manoeuvres by the cadets of the military academy of St. Cyr, there are still great tracts of it, and mysteriously still pools and lakes amongst them, where one can easily imagine oneself back in the Middle Ages. **Paimpont**, at the heart of the forest, is a pleasant little market village with a much restored abbey church on the edge of the lake; it suffers from too many day visitors in summer; and I would prefer to stay at **Mauron**, just outside the forest to the north-west. From here one can explore in all directions: south to Trecesson castle; north to St. Méen-le-Grand, where the remains of the 6th-century abbey contain some fascinating old tombs, and then east a bit to look at the severe Château de Montauban, just outside the village.

A lovely side road from Mauron to Ploërmel skirts the Paimpont forest and passes through Tréhorenteuc, the best starting place for walks to the Val sans Retour or Baranton. **Ploërmel** itself is a rather sad little place, one of the few non-strategic Breton towns to have suffered in the Second World War, but it has a couple of modest hotels near the station, the *Commerce* and the *Routiers*, and good walking country nearby, around the Etang au Duc. It also has an intriguing 16th-century church dedicated to St. Armel, the town's patron saint and founder (in the 6th century). Mostly visited for its magnificent stained-glass windows (very heavily restored and re-set) I find the church more interesting for its grotesque sculptures—around the north door, on buttresses and gables and on the windows, inside as well as outside—and for its dusty tombs of former Breton dukes.

Halfway between Ploërmel and Josselin a granite obelisk has been erected that recalls one of the more incomprehensible battles of the Breton War of Succession, when thirty warriors from each side, coming from Ploërmel and Josselin respectively, butchered one another; the Ploërmel faction, representing the eventually victorious de Montforts, were led by an English commander and roundly defeated.

One wants to take the first side road to the left after this memento to useless carnage, and cross the Oust before turning right for **Josselin**. That way, one gets a fantastic view of the castle walls rising almost from the river's edge, one of the most impressive sights in all Brittany. Its most famous owner was the warrior Olivier de Clisson, who married Marguerite de Rohan, widow of the leader of the Josselin team in the Battle of Thirty, and purchased it in 1370. When he died, it went to his wife's family, the Rohans, who have owned it ever since. The riverside facade is all that remains of de Clisson's castle, for the rest was dismantled in the 15th century to punish a Rohan who had defied the reigning Breton Duke, François II, and espoused the French cause. But François's daughter, Duchesse Anne, made handsome reparation for her father's demolition and the present castle, lurking behind the feudal walls, is in weird contrast to them: an elaborately sculptured granite facade in a mixture of flamboyant Gothic and early Renaissance styles overlaid with 19th-century restorations.

The town, which has some pleasant old streets, also boasts an important 'pardon' or religious festival, held on the second Sunday in September, centred around the church of Notre-Dame-du-Roncier, on the main square, an architectural mishmash that houses the tomb of Olivier de Clisson and his wife.

The nice *Hôtel du Château*, across the bridge from the castle, makes Josselin a good base for a day or two. North of it lies more ancient woodland, the Forêt de Lanouée, whose thickets have overgrown several traces of Roman camps. Further north again, La Trinité-Porhoët has a part-Romanesque church with some fine wood carvings, and beyond it to the east, as one circles back to Josselin, is the Trappist Abbaye de Timadeuc close to the edge of the Canal de Nantes à Brest, where the monks make cheese and show slides illustrating their daily life. South of Josselin a pleasant circuit starts with the old town of Malestroit whose St. Gilles church has twin naves in different styles, and skirts the low ridges of the Landes de Lanvaux to St. Jean-Brévelay – named, oddly enough, after an English archbishop, St. John of Beverley; the slopes to the south of it abound in megaliths. From here the road back to Josselin passes through Guéhenno with one of the few Calvaries of Haute Bretagne, earlier (1550) yet more sophisticated than those in the regions further west, and with a particularly interesting ossuary in the form of a tomb guarded by soldiers.

The last town in this section is also the main market town of central Brittany, **Pontivy**, sitting astride the Blavet river which almost marks the frontier between Haute and Basse Bretagne as it flows south to Hennebont. It owes its importance—and its formal layout—to Napoleon, who recognised its strategic importance at the heart of the province and bestowed upon it a barracks, town hall, lycée and law courts; he also reinforced its importance by canalising part of the Blavet and making it a junction on the Canal de Nantes à Brest. In gratitude, the town briefly renamed itself Napoléonville. It is a cheerful little place, with a tiny but picturesque old quarter around the church of Notre-Dame-de-la-Joie, a 15th-century Rohan castle, and plenty of canal traffic to observe at the locks.

With a sprinkling of little hotels (the *Martin* and the *Robic* are the most central) it is an excellent centre for this part of Brittany, but with the exception of the large 15th-century church at Noyal-Pontivy to the east of the town, and the little

Ste. Noyale chapel just north of it, the most interesting exploration, through the Quénécan forest to the Guerlédan lake, comes into a later chapter, and my arbitrary territorial divisions take one backwards, as it were, to the south-western corner of Brittany.

Haute Bretagne: The South

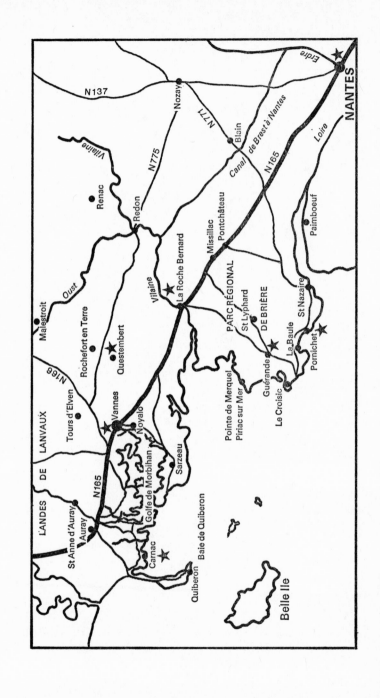

It is difficult to think of **Nantes** as a Breton city, for it has always been subject to outside influences; it was, for instance, the principal Norman base for their raids into Brittany in the 9th century. Later it became for nearly three hundred years the apex of the triangular trade route which transported French manufactured goods down the West African coast, collected West African natives there and took them to be sold as slaves in the West Indies, and finally brought back sugar cane to the Nantes refineries. Its importance as a port dwindled after the abolition of slavery and the discovery that sugar could be made from French-grown beet, and it turned its energies towards industry instead, later depending upon St. Nazaire for its sea trade, but retaining its cosmopolitan ambience—thanks partly to the Loire, along whose banks the Renaissance kings of France built their castles and brought Paris almost to its gates.

But its Breton links are strong: it was the capital of the Duchy several times in the Middle Ages, and it was the place to which Henri IV of France came to settle the vexatious religious quarrels with the signing of the Edict of Nantes in 1597. He is said to have been mightily impressed by the castle, and perhaps partly as a result Nantes had strong Royalist sympathies, though it never actually took part in any anti-revolutionary uprisings despite the appalling incident of 1793 when Royalists from its prisons were taken in barges downstream and drowned in the Loire.

And although my own first visit to Nantes was made principally to look at Le Corbusier's 'Cité Radieuse' (the then very avant-garde residential complex of flats, school, and recreational facilities that he designed for the suburb of Rézé), Nantes has more essentially Breton legacies than does Rennes. The great ducal castle is one; though it only dates from the time of Duke François II (15th century) and his daughter, Duchesse Anne, its formidable outer walls echo earlier ages. Restorations have included the re-flooding of parts of the moat, now a haven for geese and ducks and swans, and the creation of gardens around it, so it looks stunning from without.

Like Josselin, however, the internal courtyard seems to belong to a totally different building, a sophisticated grouping of facades looking inwards upon a decorative stone well topped by a wrought-iron cupola. Some interesting museums are housed here: the magnificent Art Populaire Régional collection, and the Maritime Museum (Musée de Salorges) which combines relics from the days of privateers and slavers with an intriguing collection of ancient cookery implements and cannery items—Nantes having been the birthplace of the food-canning industry in the last century.

Another museum that should not be missed, although less relevant to Brittany, is the Beaux Arts, a short detour on the route between castle and cathedral and housing masterpieces from all periods and all countries. From here one crosses the Place Maréchal Foch, passes under an old city gate, Porte St. Pierre, and arrives at the west front of the cathedral, recently re-opened after five years spent repairing fire damage. Its most interesting monument is Anne of Brittany's memorial to her mother, Marguerite of Foix, and her father, Duke François II, he who died of grief at having forfeited Breton independence. Duchesse Anne is said to have had her own heart buried in this tomb, but when the golden casket was opened it was found to be empty, and is now part of the Dobrée Museum collection.

It is a longish but pleasant walk across town to get there: through the centre of the old town and across the broad Cours-des-Cinquante-Otages, named for a bitter episode during the Second World War, which brings one to the 19th-century part of the city. Beyond the Place Royale fountain is the narrow rue Crébillon, lined with elegant shops; just off it is the fantasy-inspired Passage Pommeraie, a glazed arcade on three levels supported and embellished by curly wrought-ironwork and caryatid-like figures. Further on, Place Graslin houses the Grand Theatre and also the ravishing *La Cigale* café, a fin-de-siècle masterpiece of glazed tiles and engraved mirrors across which pre-Raphaelite ladies drift through a forest of curlicues. Alongside the rich Dobrée Museum, the former country house of the Bishops of Nantes contains a fascinating archaeological collection.

One can walk back towards the castle via the lovely formal gardens of the Cours Cambronne and thence along the Quai de la Fosse, to take in rue Kervégan, where some splendidly ornate former shipowners' mansions still exist, and then pass the little market place on the Cours Roosevelt. Just behind it, the little restaurant *Les Maraîchers* is a splendid place in which to sample the famous Nantais speciality, *beurre blanc*.

The country just south of Nantes, though technically part of Brittany, is a sort of in-between land shading into the Vendée. Olivier de Clisson originally came from these parts; the ruins of the family castle can be seen in the pretty village of the same name, at the confluence of two rivers. So did the more notorious 15th-century Breton warrior Gilles de Rais, who fought brilliantly alongside Joan of Arc and then, after her death, turned to alchemy, black magic and infanticide. He was tried and burned at the stake in Nantes, and later achieved a sort of immortality as the model for Bluebeard, the wife-killer; the ruins of his principal castle (at one time he owned great tracts of property south of the Loire) is at Tiffauges, on the Sèvre Nantaise a few miles upstream of Clisson.

Brittany also extends some way up the Loire from Nantes—as far as Ingrandes, in fact—and this section of the riverside, particularly the southern bank, is much prettier than many a more famous stretch upstream as well as being the region where Muscadet wines are grown. Its showplace is the enchanting Château de Goulaine.

Moving north-west of Nantes and avoiding, as far as possible, the noisy N165 main road (and St. Nazaire, too, unless one is passionate about shipyards – or wishes to find the very spot from which Bonnie Prince Charlie sailed for the Hebrides in 1745), one comes via the vast and much restored Calvary near Pontchâteau and the equally restored but beautifully set Château de la Bretesche, near Missillac, to the Guérande peninsula.

The D2 from Missillac is an excellent approach, for in about 8 kilometres (5 miles) it forks, and the left-hand prong traverses the marshlands of the Grande Brière, passing some of its most typical island villages. **Fédrun** is the best-known; driving slowly round it, one can appreciate the distinctive shape shared by all the marsh villages, with their cottages ranged in an inward-facing circle. At the bottom of their gardens are the waterways that criss-cross the marshes, punts moored along their banks. Once the marsh people were entirely remote, earning their living from the peat bogs and inhabiting traditional cottages of whitewashed stone with shaggy thatched roofs overgrown with damp moss. Now the proximity of St. Nazaire and of La Baule has not only given them alternative jobs nearby, but has also brought the outside world, in the form of cheap-looking new villas and coachloads of tourists, to their doors. The canals that have turned so much marshland into pasture are also eroding its character, but especially out of season the Grande Brière still has a strange, other-worldly feel, best appreciated by making a boat trip through its canals.

With no good reason for continuing to St. Nazaire, turn back at St. Malo-de-Guersac and circle the northern tip of the Grande Brière to St. Lyphard and Guérande; there are lovely views over the marshes on the way. **Guérande** is one of the few towns in France to have kept its ramparts intact; built between the 13th and 15th centuries by the de Montfort Dukes, they are more or less circular and pierced by only four gates, of which the most picturesque is the Porte-St. Michel. One can drive most of the way round the ramparts on a road formed in the 18th century by filling in the moat, and then return to the Porte-St. Michel to look first at the excellent little local folklore museum in its gatehouse and then to follow the web of narrow streets to the church of St. Aubin, almost at the dead centre of town. It has a nice double flamboyant Gothic door in the west front, and a funny little external pulpit, and some good grotesque carvings inside; opposite its south side the *Roc Maria* hotel (no restaurant, unfortunately) is housed in a former 15th-century mansion.

Due south of Guérande, past the fine 14th-century Château of Careil, is the big, wholesome-looking resort of **La Baule**, flanked by the smaller and older villages of **Le Pouliguen** and **Pornichet**, the former with a pretty little yacht-harbour at the mouth of the canal that carries the tides in to the salt marshes behind; the latter with a charming hotel, the *Fleur du Thé*. Following the corniche road which runs above the cave known as the Grotte des Korrigans ('korrigans' are the Breton equivalents of goblins, or leprechauns), one comes to **Batz**, an old town with a church dating back to the 15th century, surmounted by a later tower that is a landmark visible for miles. Balzac stayed here on several occasions writing the novel *Beatrix*, in which he described Guérande. The road goes through Batz and past the Port-Lin beach before it circles the furthest point of the peninsula and comes back to the little fishing port-cum-resort of Le Croisic. Coming inland again, the road runs clear across the chequerboard of the salt marshes to the salt-village of Saillé and here one can turn off and follow the marshes and then the coast for miles, through Piriac and up to the Pointe de Merquel, zigzagging round the inlets and promontories and watching villagers squelching across the sands at low tide in search of mussels and clams, until the Vilaine estuary puts a stop to coast-hugging and leads one back inland again to **La Roche-Bernard.**

This is an excellent place to pause for a night or two and explore a little further up the Vilaine valley, for La Roche-Bernard has no fewer than three small hotels which produce better than average cuisine at lower than average prices: the *Deux Magots*, the *Bretagne* and the *Bretonne*. Two of them get the *Red Michelin Guide* accolade for *repas soignés à prix modérés* so the patron saint of La Roche-Bernard must have had a soft spot for impoverished eaters. It is surprisingly un-touristy, too, despite its attractive situation perched above the splendid bridge that carries the N165 westwards, and some nice crooked old houses crouch around its Place du Boufflay.

The prettiest road to Redon is on the other side of the estuary, where a succession of little lanes parallel the steep Vilaine valley, opening unexpectedly on to superb views every two or three kilometres. **Redon**, at the junction of the Vilaine and the Nantes-Brest canal, is a little market town with a very long history indeed: there has been an abbey here since the 9th century, when it was established under Nominoë, Brittany's first Duke, and although the present church of St. Sauveur dates only from the 13th century, its lantern tower is a century and more older and one of the few Romanesque monuments in Brittany. Across from it is a free-standing Gothic tower, cut off from the rest of the abbey buildings by a fire in 1780; the 18th-century monastery buildings alongside the church now house a college. There are some charming old houses behind this, along the Quai St. Jaques, and also along the Grande-rue which runs from the market square down to the main road.

One can more or less follow the Vilaine up to Rennes by using side roads, but the most interesting point is long before that, at **Langon**, a tiny village sheltering the oldest complete building in Brittany. The now disused Chapelle Ste. Agathe, standing opposite the village church, dates back to Gallo-Roman times when it was probably a sanctuary of Venus—a faded and damaged fresco, quite recently uncovered, shows the goddess rising from a sea of fishes. In the 12th century it was altered, by this time having been dedicated to an otherwise unknown 'St. Vener'; some five hundred years later it was re-dedicated to St. Agatha, who attained sainthood by sur-viving a brutal mastectomy and thus became venerated by women with breast afflictions. It is a strange little place, surrounded by trees and scattered menhirs, and well away from any main tourist route.

Cutting westwards across country from Langon, via Renac, a hamlet called simply La Bataille, together with a stone cross on the edge of it and a modern statue of Nominoë, together recall the battle by which Brittany severed itself from Carol-ingian rule. Another important battleground lies further west still, but before arriving there one wants to pause at the enchanting small village of **Rochefort-en-Terre**, its little granite houses straggling along a ridge of the Landes de Lanvaux, below the remains of an old castle, much restored, and with a pleasant 16th-century church. Beyond it, there is nothing but a modest stone pyramid to remind one that Questembert saw the last great battle between Duke Alain Barbe-Torte and the Norman invaders in 938; it is said that of the fifteen-hundred-strong raiding force fewer than five hundred escaped. Today **Questembert** is a cheerful little town with an old covered market and a Calvary in its churchyard, plus the splendid restaurant of the *Hôtel de Bretagne*, all of which need to be pursued with some determination, since the one-way traffic system seems designed to keep people well away from town.

From Questembert it is probably best to go straight to Vannes, or to one of the quieter places just south or east of it

(Conleau, Theix, Noyalo) and base oneself there for a few days, because there is a tremendous amount to see around the Gulf of Morbihan and no direct connection across the narrow strait between its two enfolding arms; consequently there is a lot of tiresome retracing of tracks if one is not strategically placed at its centre.

Vannes itself, home of the first Dukes of Brittany and intermittently the Duchy's capital, is a tourist-conscious little town, which is not to denigrate it; except at the height of the summer season this can be a positive advantage. After a succession of nights spent in quieter locales, a bit of town-centre bustle around a hotel like the *Manche Océan* might be quite welcome. Vannes is, moreover, an exceedingly pretty little town, with a canalised port leading like a driveway from the gulf to the very foot of its well-kept ramparts. Above them, old streets lined with high-gabled, timber-framed houses, projecting slightly over the pavements, lead to the oddly lopsided Cathédrale St. Pierre, which took nearly six hundred years to complete and is consequently an extraordinary jumble.

Within it is the tomb of an Anglo-Spanish monk, St. Vincent Ferrer; he was summoned to Brittany by one of the early de Montfort Dukes, Jean the Wise, who during his reign in the early 15th century not only consolidated Breton administration but also established a navy that went to the aid of the rebellious Welshman, Owen Glendower. St. Vincent Ferrer being the foremost preacher of the age, and Duke Jean being determined to improve his subjects' piety, the great missionary was invited to Vannes where, after two years' passionate evangelism, he died in 1419. Although his sojourn in Brittany was so short, he made a strong impression, and the religious revival he generated is manifest in scores of Calvaries and small churches built during the following seventy-odd years.

Behind the cathedral, a steep little street leads down to the

Postern Gate, at the end of the ramparts, and below this is a view of some odd 16th-century timber-framed wash-houses which are still in use; seldom is there no washing flapping on the lines beside them. Coming back towards the irregularly shaped main square, Place des Lices, which seethes with colour and activity on market days, an ancient house at one side of it is known as the House of Vannes; from its walls two carved wooden figures grin fiendishly down on the scene below. Behind it is a 15th-century mansion housing an important archaeological collection of finds from the whole Morbihan region; behind that again, in the 17th-century Chamber of Commerce building, is the comparatively new Oyster Museum (Musée de l'Huitre) which throws some interesting sidelights on the life-style—and fashionability—of the monarch of molluscs.

One can radiate out in several directions from Vannes. Inland of it are the moorlands of the Landes de Lanvaux, wonderful walking country, and, on the way there, the romantic half-ruined former castle of Largoët, more popularly known as les Tours d'Elven, where the future Henry VII of England spent two years in prison. Nearby is the little village of St. Avé with a typically rural Calvary and some pleasant manor houses.

To the south and east the Rhuys peninsula enjoys an amazingly gentle climate: I have wandered along its southern beaches in February and even been tempted to bathe. Near the sea on this shore is the Château de Suscinio, built as a summer residence by an early 13th-century duke. It has survived many a battering in the intervening centuries and was partly demolished for building-stone after the Revolution. Further along this same southern shore is the monastery of St. Gildas-de-Rhuys, founded in the 6th century, whose most famous abbot was Pierre Abélard (who was intensely unhappy there, separated from his Héloïse and hated by the monks for the scandal he had caused).

Off the tip of this peninsula, now occupied by tiny Port-Navalo, was fought the naval battle in which Caesar's ships destroyed those of the Gaulish Veneti tribe, and Caesar is supposed to have watched the conflict from the tumulus of Tumiac. Coming back to Vannes by the road which skirts the Morbihan side of the peninsula, one passes through the big village of Sarzeau, and the Château de Kerlévénan, its Classical facade quite visible from the road.

Another fascinating trip from Vannes is the *promenade en bateau* around the islands of the Gulf. There are hundreds of them, many invisible at low tide; others big enough for villages; several with megalithic remains. The two biggest are the **Ile d'Arz** and the **Ile aux Moines**, both with restaurants on them; the one on the Ile aux Moines is especially popular. But the most interesting of the Morbihan islands is reached not from Vannes but from Larmor-Baden on the shore opposite; it is **Gavrinis**, site of one of the greatest of Breton megalithic monuments. Under a rocky tumulus overgrown with weedy tufts are a huge covered gallery with carved supports and a burial chamber whose ceiling is one enormous rectangular stone. A noble grave constructed in distant antiquity for someone of enormous importance; who it was, we shall probably never know, but simply contemplating it seems to evoke the echoes of long-unheard sighs.

Coming back from Gavrinis and Larmor-Baden towards Auray, there is a lovely view as one crosses high over the estuary of Le Bono, with the tiny port full of fishing craft below, and then one turns sharply off for St. Goustan, the oldest quarter of the attractive little port town of **Auray**, where Benjamin Franklin landed briefly in 1778 en route for Nantes and Paris to solicit help for his fellow revolutionaries. A steep and picturesque little corner, half encircled by the river, it is joined by a bridge to the newer part of the town on the other side. Due north of Auray is the battlefield, overlooked by a much rebuilt Carthusian monastery, where in 1364 the last battle of the Breton War of Succession was fought, in which Jean de Montfort triumphed over Charles of Blois and du Guesclin, and Olivier de Clisson lost an eye. Just beyond is the great pilgrimage centre of Ste. Anne-d'Auray where, in 1625, a peasant unearthed at the saint's command a statue that had lain buried for centuries. The present basilica was built in the last century and its 'pardons' draw huge crowds.

From here one must inevitably turn south, to **Carnac** and the rows of megalithic monuments that stand like ranks of petrified soldiers in the moorlands behind it. Roughly contemporary with the Minoan monuments of Crete, though far cruder, they nevertheless strike a chill, especially when seen after the coachloads have departed and the setting sun throws their ghostly shadows across the scrubland. There are dozens more dolmens and menhirs scattered inland of this part of Morbihan, behind Locmariaquer and La Trinité as well as Carnac, their beaches and little yachting ports and trim villas and hotels and pine-bordered boulevards and bucket-and-spade shops all worlds away from legend-shrouded megaliths. Some of the finds from these prehistoric sites are housed in the little museum in **Carnac-Ville** (hotels: *Tumulus* or *Lann Roz*), which is just behind **Carnac-Plage** (hotel *Les Genêts*, near the beach). Also in Carnac-Ville is a charming little church with a relief of St. Cornély, patron saint of cattle, smirking impishly from between a pair of oxen.

Stretching away to the south of Carnac is the long thin Quiberon peninsula, once an island and now linked to the mainland by a strip of land hardly wider than the road. Its Atlantic coast is wild and studded with the sort of rocks which to some people inevitably resemble faces or animals or birds and which to me are equally inevitably just rocks; nonetheless the views are fine and the breezes bracing. At the tip of the peninsula is a large thalassotherapy institute, one of the first in France and reverently spoken of by those who devote proper consideration to matters of health. There is also the small port of Quiberon, from which boats leave for the southern Breton islands, but I am ashamed to say that I have never thought the waters calm enough for a poor sailor like myself to venture upon, though one day I should like to visit Belle-Ile. The main road from Quiberon back to the mainland borders the duller eastern coast of the peninsula, dotted with villas and tiny resorts.

Basse Bretagne: The South

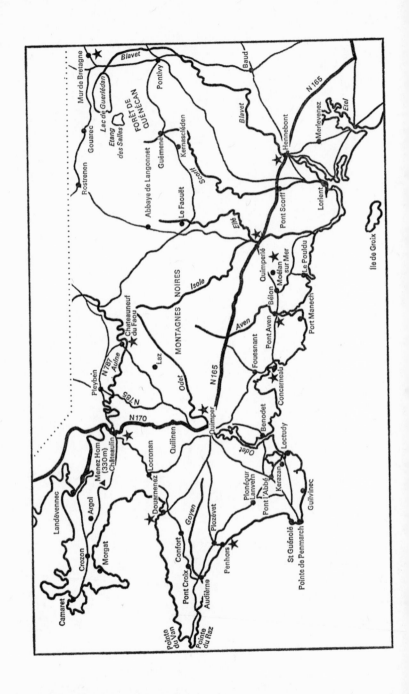

An invisible line runs roughly inland from Quiberon, through Baud, paralleling the uncertain course of the Blavet up to Pontivy and beyond; it is the division between Haute and Basse Bretagne. Some guide-books put it a little further to the east, and include half of the Morbihan Gulf in Basse Bretagne; some put it slightly further west. Its exact location is not important; what does matter is to be aware that once past this blurred frontier one is in a much more foreign country, where people react in a less predictably French manner, where ancient superstitions and beliefs are still a real influence on daily life, and where many, even now, still speak Breton as their first language.

This is not immediately apparent, of course; to the tourist in a hurry it may not be apparent at all. But there is a difference, and one might as well be prepared for it.

Coming back from the coast towards the lake-like Etel estuary, it is worth making a slight detour, before crossing the soaring suspension bridge, for a look at the tiny fishing village of **St. Cado,** partly built on an islet connected by a causeway to the mainland. Apart from making a charming picture, especially at high tide, it also hides among its cottages a tiny former Templars' chapel whose simple Romanesque lines are echoed by the far more modern Calvary outside it.

Across the bridge, from which there are wonderful views up the estuary and down, towards its narrow, steep-sided outlet to the sea, **Merlevenez** stands at the next major crossroads. Here is another of Brittany's rare Romanesque churches, this one complete with elegant geometrical carvings around its arches. And here one must decide whether to go on to Hennebont, or to turn right instead for Baud and the wonderful inland country beyond. Or to do both, making **Hennebont** a

detour. There is a splendid luxurious château-hotel just outside
it, the *Château de Locguénolé*, which is an undeniable, if expensive, attraction, but the town itself was so badly destroyed
when the Americans occupied it during their siege of Lorient
(which remained in German hands until 8 May 1945), that it
has few antiquities left. Its connection with a much earlier siege
is fascinating, though, for in 1341 during the War of Succession
the wife of the eventual victor, Jean de Montfort (he was in
prison at the time), was fighting desperately to hold off Charles
of Blois and the French. Leaving her baby son, later to become
Duke Jean IV, inside the castle, she ventured out one night at
the head of three hundred hand-picked troops and set fire to
the enemy camp—a feat which earned her the name of
Jeanne de la Flamme. Even so, her position was perilous, so
by one of those oddly courteous agreements which occasionally interrupted these sanguineous battles, she was given three
days in which to await reinforcements or surrender. Luckily,
an English fleet sailed up the estuary just in time. Nothing
remains of her castle; only fragments of the town ramparts and
one splendid gate, the Porte du Broerech. The 16th-century
church of Notre-Dame-du-Paradis, with its massive belfry
and steeple, is also worth seeing.

Inland, at the extreme western end of the Landes de Lanvaux
uplands, the chief interest of the little town of **Baud** is the
larger-than-life-sized statue of a woman which stands above a
fountain just west of the town. She is of very ancient origins,
possibly Egyptian, possibly Roman. For years she was hidden
in a mountain grave near Castennec, between Baud and Pontivy, perhaps buried by St. Gildas as a heathen image. Even
after her discovery she was 'deposed' and flung into the river
several times, but each time the villagers, whose wives believed
firmly in her gynaecological powers, reinstated her. Finally the
ecclesiastical authorities had her destroyed, and the present
statue is an 18th-century copy, known not as the 'Witch of La

Couarde', which was her ancient name, but as the 'Venus of Quinipily'.

There are some charming little places between Pontivy and Baud, along the course of the Blavet: the eminence of Cast-ennec, with road and river alike twisting round it, where St. Gildas-de-Rhuys once inhabited a cave (and buried the original Venus); pretty St. Nicholas-des-Eaux; St. Nicodème, another picturesque hamlet with a delightful flamboyant Gothic chapel and fountain; Melrand, a sleepy Breton town with several old granite houses, Bieuzy, and finally **Quelven**. This hamlet has an immensely popular statue of the Virgin in its 16th-century chapel; she swings open to reveal twelve reliefs of the life of Christ sculpted within her. Her 'pardon', or religious festival on August 15, is well attended by people from all the surrounding villages and, eclipsed as it is by the greater August 15 'pardons' at Perros-Guirec and Plougastel-Daoulas, has a genuinely rural atmosphere.

North of Pontivy, still following the Blavet, **Stival**'s parish church was formerly the chapel of St. Meriadec; it has some fine stained-glass windows and frescoes and also, more interesting still, the saint's 8th-century bronze bell, which is kept in the sacristy. North again, **Mur-de-Bretagne** is another delightful stopping place, for its *Auberge de la Gran' Maison* has truly marvellous food. Conveniently, the huge artificial lake of Guerlédan is close by, with lots of lovely walks and views along its shores and the Quénécan forest at its south-western end. Here, too, are the ruins of the Abbey of Bon-Repos, founded in the 12th century; the ruins of a Rohan castle dreaming above the Etang des Salles, with a nearby farmhouse that was once part of the castle; Les Forges des Salles, with the present château, and, just north again, some lovely heathland cut by the course of the Blavet as it rushes into the lake.

Gouarec and Rostrenen, the latter a market town with an

interesting church porch, are both pleasant enough but not really worth lingering in, to my mind; from one or the other I would start back for the coast again; this part of Brittany positively forces one to zigzag back and forth a good deal. This time one is joining the course of the Scorff for part of the way, passing through Guéméné-sur-Scorff, where a very few traces of walls are all that is left of a once great castle, and continuing down to Kernascléden. The church of this tiny village is rich in beautiful flamboyant Gothic carvings and well-restored 16th-century frescoes populated with agonised faces; the Danse Macabre and Vision of Hell are particularly shiver-inducing. Just south of here, between a lake and a forest, is the former Château of Pont-Calleck, now a children's home; and about 16 kilometres (10 miles) westwards is the big village of **Le Faouët**, in the middle of some lovely country, with a 16th-century covered market of timber supported on granite pillars in its big shady square. It is surrounded with monuments: the chapel of Ste. Barbe, in a rocky hillside hollow, connected by an imposing flight of marble steps to the buildings on the terrace above; the lonely St. Nicholas chapel, with an interesting rood screen, just off the Priziac road; and the Abbey of Langonnet, with a lovely 13th-century chapter house among its less interesting buildings, to the north of Priziac. A pretty road follows the Ellé from here back to Le Faouët, and just south of it is the most interesting chapel of all, St. Fiacre, with a 15th-century wooden rood screen most miraculously carved with grotesque figures and patterns of lacy intricacy.

About 18 kilometres (11 miles) south of here is **Quimperlé**, its old quarter hugged between the Ellé and the Isole, with the curiously shaped church of Ste. Croix at its centre. Modelled on the Church of the Holy Sepulchre in Jerusalem, it has a lovely Romanesque apse and crypt; the rest of the church was damaged when the belfry collapsed in the last century and has been rebuilt. There are some fine old houses with projecting upper storeys in the streets around it and, across the river and up the opposite hill, the beautiful Gothic church of St. Michel.

A delightful, quiet little hotel, the *Hermitage* stands on the edge of the forest just south of Quimperlé, and another rather grander one, *Les Moulins du Duc*, a bit further afield at **Moëlan-sur-Mer** (actually not 'sur mer' at all), consists of cottages grouped around an old mill. Neither is cheap, but both are strategically placed for exploring the coast. I do not suggest that anyone should go to Lorient, for although founded by Louis XIV's clever Norman minister, Colbert, as the base for the East India Company, it was more or less razed at the end of the Second World War and is now entirely modern. But the coast is lovely south of Le Pouldu, and to the west some of the best Breton cider comes from around the little fishing port of Doëlan. Further west still is the little Bélon estuary, almost as full of sailing boats as it is of oysters; Riec-sur-Bélon, Kerfavy-les-Pins, and Bélon itself are the best places for oyster feasts.

So, indeed, is **Pont-Aven,** where the old mill that is now the *Moulin Rosmadec* restaurant announces in the *Red Michelin Guide* that its specialities are *tous les poissons*. Also known for its uniquely shaped Breton *coiffe*, or starched linen and lace head-dress, this pleasant old town has a further claim to fame in having been a haunt of Paul Gauguin: he founded a painting school there in 1887 and stayed two years, broken by an un-happy interlude with Van Gogh at Arles, before moving on, via Paris, to seek true simplicity in the South Pacific. Many a Pont-Aven scene will be familiar to admirers of Gauguin's work, including the 16th-century wooden Christ in the Kermalo chapel, and the Calvary of Nizon.

Still hugging the coast en route to Quimper, **Concarneau** is primarily a tuna fishing port, but its Ville Close, built on an island in the middle of the port, is unique. Wrapped in ram-parts that were begun in the 14th century and finished by the great 17th-century military architect, Vauban (a pathway runs round them), its network of tiny alleys is redolent of fishy smells and mediaeval atmosphere. It celebrates its fascinating Festival of the Blue Fishing Nets (*Fête des Filets Bleus*) in August, and has an equally fascinating fish museum which contains specimens of the earliest sardine containers. After all of which the only possible thing to do is cross back to the main part of town and have fish soup in a quayside restaurant: that of the *Grand Hôtel* for a superlative version, or at *Chez Armande* for something more modest.

From here, a pretty road skirts the bay to Fouesnant, by way of La Forêt-Fouesnant—all rich cider country. La Forêt also has a fine 'parish close' and is a thriving resort, though not so popular as either Bénodet or Beg-Meil, both with vast and cleaner beaches. But out of season, especially, when the resorts are half empty, I would prefer to stay in **Quimper** itself (at the *Tour d'Auvergne*) for it is an endearing town, full of good-humoured bustle, where on market days one still sees sturdy old ladies in something like traditional costume: not *coiffes*, normally, but some sort of head-covering, and huge bunchy skirts belted tightly at the waist, woollen shawls and wooden sabots. All around the market place, which is just west of the cathedral, are lovely old streets of half-timbered buildings, many of their facades also protected with slates, sagging picturesquely against one another. Even the cathedral, begun in the 13th century and laboriously built over the following two, with spires that are later still, is slightly lopsided thanks to soil subsidence. The west facade is graced with a statue of the city's 6th-century founder, King Gradlon, mounted on a horse: his original capital of Ys was engulfed by the sea because, according to legend, of the enslavement of his daughter by the Devil. In his sorrow, the King was comforted by St. Corentin, who in turn was sustained by a miraculous fish: every day he ate half of it and returned the rest to the river where it became whole again in time for the next day's meal.

St. Corentin was Quimper's first bishop and the cathedral is named for him; it has some beautiful 15th-century stained glass in the upper windows and scenes from the life of the saint are carved around the pulpit. In the former Bishop's Palace hard by the cathedral is a perfectly splendid Breton museum containing furniture, costumes and pottery.

That pottery is Quimper's chief industry is obvious everywhere as one wanders along the quaysides of the river and along charming rue Kéréon towards the bridge over the Steir; it has been hand-made in the suburb of Locmaria since the 17th century and still keeps alive its Rouen-inspired traditional designs, though new ones appear from time to time. The other Quimper speciality is *crêpes dentelles*, crisp thin pancakes, slightly sweet, rolled up like fat cigars and often packed in charmingly painted tin boxes.

Quimper is a perfect centre for excursions in surrounding Cornouaille (its name echoing that of England's Cornwall, from which so many early Bretons came). Its geographical position is convenient, for one thing; for another, it is an exceptionally nice place to return to; after three or four days there, people in the streets nod as to an old resident. The 16-kilometre (10-mile) boat trip down the Odet estuary, now wide and still as a lake, now narrow and twisting, its west bank lined with fine châteaux, takes about an hour and a half to reach Bénodet. From there one can cross the bridge to the prettier fishing village of Ste. Marine, and sit in a café on the harbour front admiring the panorama of little craft before returning to Quimper either by bus or water.

West of the Odet is the stubby peninsula of the *pays* Bigouden, home of one of the most typical of Breton *coiffes*, with its capital at **Pont l'Abbé**—where a lovely array of these *coiffes* are on display at the Musée Bigouden in the 14th–17th-century fortress. Down the estuary, past the Château de Kérazan (containing an embroidery school endowed by

Joseph Astor in 1929) is **Loctudy**—whose monks built the original bridge at Pont l'Abbé that gave the town its name. Faced by the long finger of the Ile Tudy, it is a delightful little fishing harbour and its church, lurking behind an uninviting 18th-century facade, is a glorious and rare example of Breton Romanesque. A tall ancient menhir in its courtyard has had a cross carved out of its tip at some later date, giving it an oddly forlorn look of not belonging.

West again from Loctudy the landscape begins to take on a more windswept, Atlantic character; detour southward and follow the minor road from Guilvinec to the Pointe de Penmarch and the change is noticeable. At the tip of the peninsula the tall Eckmuhl lighthouse (marvellous views from the top) rises from the reefs with a 15th-century chapel alongside; north of it the road passes another small chapel before arriving at St. Guénolé, against whose rocks the Atlantic breaks in fantastic pillars of spume. There is the little prehistoric museum of Finistère on the road beyond it, towards Anse de la Torche beach, and after this one can curl back inland to Penmarch itself, centre of a region that has declined sadly in prosperity over the last five hundred years, first due to the disappearance of the rich cod shoals from its waters, then thanks to the depredations of the 16th-century pirate, La Fontenelle, who ravaged this entire coast from his island base opposite Douarnez. But it has some fine relics of its better days: a ruined 15th-century castle with a fat round keep, and the flamboyant Gothic church of St. Nona.

From here one wants to zigzag north across the moors to the lonely chapel of Notre-Dame-de-Tronoën, on a little hill that commands the desolate bay of Audierne; its Calvary, rising from a rectangular granite base, its details blurred by the Atlantic gales, is the oldest in Brittany and dates from the late 15th century. From here, the road back to Quimper is via Plonéour-Lanvern and the ruined chapel of Notre-Dame-de-

Languivea beyond it.

There are more chapels on the stretch between Plonéour-Lanvern and Plozévet, further north: Languidou, also in ruins; Plovan, with good modern glass; and **Penhors**, which has one of the most important 'pardons' of the region—and also a modest restaurant, the *Breiz Armor*, with immense views. Plozévet is on the main road from Quimper to the Pointe du Raz; it has an interesting church with a fountain beside it. Although the coast beyond is impressive, it is probably more rewarding to turn inland here and make a detour via the pretty chapel of La Trinité to Confort, whose 16th-century church has an unusual prayer wheel hung with twelve bells that are rung to invoke favours from the Virgin. From here one can come down the estuary of the Goyen via Pont-Croix, piled in terraces above the river and huddled about its charming church of Notre-Dame-de-Roscudon, to Audierne, spilling on to wide quaysides covered in nets and lobster-traps. This is at the base of the wild Pointe du Raz peninsula (detour first to the rich little chapel of St. Tugen, just west of it), with any number of dauntingly vertiginous cliff paths for the courageous to negotiate and some menacing outlooks, despite the scatter of restaurants and villas and souvenir kiosks. Below the rocky eminences of the Pointe du Raz and its lighthouse, a little road wanders north past the Baie des Trépassés (Bay of the Dead) whence the bodies of priests were in ancient times ferried out to burial on the Ile de Sein, offshore. It is one of the spots claimed as the original site of the drowned city of Ys, and ends at the lesser peninsula of the Pointe-du-Van, with one tiny chapel. From here one can come back along the north shore, past the wonderfully situated bird sanctuary of Cap Sizun (particularly interesting in nesting time) to **Douarnez**. A whitewashed fishing port at the mouth of the Pouldavid, one should walk round it to enjoy the view across to Ile Tristan, the former pirate's lair, and the robust, salty atmosphere—particularly on the Rosmeur quayside—and then eat hugely of fish at the *Hôtel de France* before returning to Quimper via the enchanting village of **Locronan**, named after the Irish saint, Ronan, who arrived there at the end of the 5th century. Its setting is wonderful, with St. Ronan's hill rising behind it, and its main square is a gem of 16th-century stone houses dominated by the big church and chapel of Le Pénity. Behind it and down the hill is another church, even more attractive: Notre-Dame-de-Bonne-Nouvelle, with a typically Breton Calvary and fountain. The 'pardons' of Locronan are based on the penitential walks made by St. Ronan, the one taking place every sixth year (1983 will be the next) being the biggest and most elaborate. There is also an exceptionally famous August 'pardon' at Ste. Anne-la-Palud, near the coast just north of Locronan – whose beach, incidentally, rejoices in one of the most luxurious hotels in Brittany.

Leaving Quimper for the last time on this theoretical tour, and moving towards the north-western corner of Brittany, the road to Châteaulin passes two charming rural churches with Calvaries: Quilinen, a 16th-century beauty, and St. Venec, rather battered. **Châteaulin**, a great mecca for salmon fishermen, sits on both banks of the Aulne in the heart of an extraordinarily pretty valley; as it is also favoured with an inn (the *Ducs de Lin*) that does remarkably good food, being especially generous with the early fruit and vegetables grown hereabouts, it makes a good stopping place. Up the Aulne and slightly north of it, **Pleyben** has one of the most monumental 'parish closes' in all Brittany, with a Calvary on a massive vaulted base, a towering 16th-century church, and an ossuary that ante-dates both, all overhung with trees and reached through a huge triumphal arch. From Pleyben one can continue a satisfying circuit up the Aulne valley by taking the minor roads to prettily situated **Châteauneuf-du-Faou** (with a good simple restaurant, the *Relais de Cornouaille*), crossing the valley to the remote, early 16th-century chapel of Notre-Dame-du-Crann, and coming back through the foothills of the Montagnes Noires, the Forêt de Laz and the high-perched village of the same name.

West of Châteaulin, the modest swelling of the Menez-Hom, at 330 metres one of Brittany's higher mountains, guards the little Crozon peninsula, sticking like a forked dragon's tongue into the gap between the jaw-like masses to the north and south of it. Coming down from the Menez-Hom viewpoint, past the little chapel of Ste. Marie, it is worth pausing at the hamlet of **Argol**, in the centre of the peninsula; the statue of King Gradlon on horseback in the parish close is neither old nor particularly noteworthy artistically, but it reminds one not only that his drowned city of Ys may lie beneath the waters of the nearby bays, but also how entwined are legend, religion and history in this part of Brittany.

Beyond Argol is Crozon, the little town that gives the peninsula its name, and beyond that, circling in a clockwise direction, a perfect succession of wild, sea-washed panoramas, starting from the pretty and popular little resort of Morgat and going round cape after cape, cove after sandy cove and promontory after promontory, every one opening up a different yet typically Breton view. Enemy fleets, British, Dutch and Spanish, have hurled themselves at various points along this jagged coast and been thrown back, but Vauban's 17th-century fortifications have been superseded by the remnants of Hitler's Atlantic Wall. The little port of Camaret is an important lobster fishing centre as well as a modest resort; Le Fret, at the base of the Pointe des Espagnols, was where Jeanne de Navarre, widow of a Breton duke, set sail in 1402 to become the second wife of England's Henry IV; now it is a day-excursion centre also linked by boat to Brest.

Coming back along the north side of the peninsula, the sweet village of **Landévennec** lies on a comma-shaped promontory at the mouth of the Aulne; almost at its tip, in a wooded setting, are the scant Romanesque remains of the famous 5th-century abbey, founded by St. Guénolé, where King Gradlon was buried. For five hundred years it was immensely powerful, both politically and spiritually, and even its destruction by the Normans in the 10th century only kept the monks away temporarily. It was pulled down after the Revolution, however, and the new one stands uphill of it.

Basse Bretagne: The North

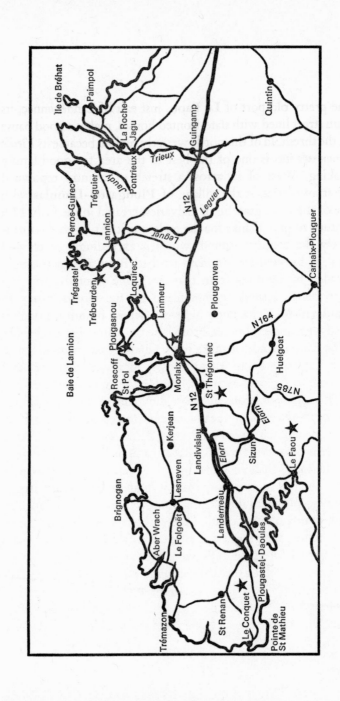

The pretty old port of **Le Faou**, just east of Landévennec, its main street lined with slate-fronted houses, makes a good pause on the threshold of this north-westerly region, because its *Vieille Renommée* inn is one of the best in the area for good family cooking. West of it, across a stretch of country renowned for strawberries, is the village of **Plougastel-Daoulas** with one of the most graceful of Calvaries, created in the early 17th century to give thanks for the ending of the plague. Unfortunately the country around, which is exceedingly pretty and rural, is bisected by the main road to Brest and increasingly invaded by fugitives from that city. One wants to give it a wide berth, I think, going inland up the Elorn estuary to **Landerneau**, a charming old town whose beautiful bridge is lined with ancient houses. From here one can either circle back to Le Faou inland; or make for a suitable base from which to tour the remarkable 'parish closes' of this region; or, as I propose to do, go westwards first for the Aber country.

This is part of Léon, and quite different from Cornouaille to the south, with rolling heathland punctuated by the occasional cornfield and lone menhir covering a low central plateau. At its centre is the old town of St. Renan, and its shores are indented by the long, shallow gulfs, or abers, that give the region its name. Islands spatter away from it in all directions, the largest and best-known of them being Ouessant, or Ushant. It lacks the stark drama of Cornouaille; the compilers of Michelin maps, who bestow their highest accolade of a green 'edge' upon roads that border forests or cliffs, have been stingy with their green ink here, except for the region around the Aber-Wrach and the Aber-Benoit. But it has a poetic, melancholic sort of appeal. A leisurely circuit, broken perhaps beneath the radio masts of Le Conquet, for the *bar au beurre blanc* at the Pointe Ste. Barbe is well worth making. There are some superb views coming north from Le Conquet to Trémazan and Aber-Wrach and one that is grimmer: of the angular wreck of the *Amoco Cadiz* which spewed oil on to so many innocent beaches in 1978. The beaches have now been lovingly cleaned, but after Aber-Wrach I would turn inland anyway, to **Le Folgoët**, the 'Fool of the Wood', whose large church was built by the victorious de Montforts in the early 15th century. It commemorates the miracle of the simpleton who lived in a hollow tree and begged for his food, uttering only the words 'Ave Maria', and from whose grave a lily sprang bearing the same words. An enormous open space surrounds the church, accentuating its size and the inequality of its two west front towers. It is a lovely sight from without (the fountain behind the main altar should not be missed), and within is one of the most exquisite rood screens of Brittany, carved from the local granite.

Lesneven, a couple of kilometres away, is a nice old town with a couple of good little inns, but I would prefer to base myself further east for a few days, at the delightful little *Auberge de St. Thégonnec*, just south-west of Morlaix. It stands very near to one of the most wonderful of Breton 'parish closes' and within easy reach are half a dozen more: Guimiliau, Lampaul-Guimiliau, Ploudiry, la Martyre, Sizun, Locmélar, Pleyber-Christ, Plougonven, and Commana in the Monts d'Arrée foothills. They date from the 16th and 17th centuries and all are different, but it would be hopelessly repetitive to try and describe each one. Almost all are composed of the essential features of triumphal arch, Calvary, and ossuary, grouped beside the parish church and its cemetery; all are richly sculpted with marvellous agonised figures and faces and a wealth of decorative detail; together they make an enthralling study. So, indeed, do the churches themselves: the rood beam at Lampaul-Guimiliau, the pulpit at St. Thégonnec, the font at Guimiliau—and its great south porch which, like that of

Landivisiau and many others in Brittany, was used as a meeting place for the parish elders.

As a change from 'parish closes', the Château of Kerjean lies just north of Landivisiau: a vastly fortified *enceinte* surrounded by walls and bastions within which is a surprising Renaissance courtyard surrounded by elegantly decorative buildings. It contains some beautiful Breton furniture and is associated with a nice story about a pretty and virtuous châtelaine who demurely locked four would-be seducers (who were trying to win a bet with her husband about her purity) into a room, one by one, and there set them to weaving cloth.

Another pleasant alternative to 'parish closes' is to go inland across the moors and through the woods to **Huelgoat**, a popular little town surrounded by pools and streams and trees and rocks and a good centre for walks and picnics; beyond it is the mellow little town of **Carhaix-Plouguer**, also set in lovely country full of interesting villages. It was once a Roman settlement and its most famous son of more recent years was the soldier-scholar La Tour d'Auvergne, born Théophile-Malo Corret, whose passion was the study of the Breton language.

The three charming towns of Morlaix, St. Pol-de-Léon and Roscoff are also within easy striking distance of St. Thégonnec; **Morlaix**, cradled in the steep-sided estuary of its river, with the railway viaduct soaring over it, is immensely picturesque: yachts and other pleasure craft are crammed along its quaysides and its streets, sloping up the hillsides, are lined with pretty old houses. Anne of Brittany visited Morlaix on a pilgrimage round her Duchy in 1505, when she gave thanks at numerous stopping places for the recovery of her husband Louis XII from an illness, and the house where she stayed is the town's pride and joy. Some twenty years later members of an English invading force managed to get very drunk in the cellars of the undefended town, whose more stalwart citizens were absent that day; they became so drunk that they were easily trounced when the warriors returned. Apart from the old gabled houses and cobbled alleyways, the church of Ste. Mélanie is particularly fine, and the largish *Hôtel de l'Europe* is conveniently placed at the heart of the town for sightseeing.

St. Pol-de-Léon is a busy market town, the centre of a region famed for its artichokes, onions and cauliflowers; it also boasts two of the most typical and impressive Breton Gothic buildings: the cathedral and the Kreisker chapel. The cathedral, although the oldest of Breton bishoprics, is a cathedral no longer, but it is extraordinarily beautiful—with its Coutances-inspired proportions, its marvellous rose window in the transept and its beautiful 16th-century choir stalls. The Kreisker, on the other hand, is renowned chiefly for its miraculously slender and graceful belfry which, together with the towers of the former cathedral, dominate the flat countryside for miles around.

Roscoff, just north of St. Pol, is one of the terminals for the Brittany Ferries' cross-Channel boat services. It was also the terminal for a little girl's first voyage in 1548: the five-year-old Mary Stuart, Queen of Scots, landed here on her way to her betrothal with the ill-fated, future François II of France. She is said to have spent a night in one of the old houses that still stand in the appealing little grey town. Two hundred years later her descendant, Bonnie Prince Charlie, also landed here at the end of his flight from Scotland. Now it is the starting point for the dwindling band of bicycle-borne onion sellers who cross to Britain in the autumn with their handlebars wreathed in beautifully plaited ropes of silvery-gold vegetables. Nowadays, too, Roscoff is an important centre of the French Marine Biology Institute and also offers thalassotherapy facilities; thanks to its very mild climate its many hotels are steadily patronised the year round—though no one has yet claimed to equal the age of the great fig tree, propped up at scores of strategic points, that was planted early in the 17th century and still produces hundreds of kilos of fruit.

Of the coastline from Aber-Wrach eastwards, through Brignogan and Carantec and **Plougasnou** (the *Hôtel de France* here is very sweet) and Locquirec, one can say no more than that it is typically Breton—sand and cliffs and strangely shaped rocks and a convoluted coastline that has overcome the 1978 oil-spill and never fails to enchant. The same can be said for the resorts that circle the jagged outlines of the coast between Locquirec and St. Brieuc; this is one of the few areas where I might base myself by the sea and explore from the outside in, so to speak. Apart from the fact that most roads have to go through either **Lannion** (which has a good deal of character and is overlooked by a lofty Templars' church) or **Guingamp** (a shade less character, being bigger, but with the extremely interesting Notre-Dame-de-Bon-Secours, half Gothic and half Renaissance), the inland countryside is almost as accessible from the coast as vice-versa. I would choose a good hotel at Tré-beurden or Trégastel on the coast: the *Lan-Kerellec* at **Tré-beurden** is luxurious while the *Grève Blanche* at **Trégastel** is more modest. I have nothing against Perros-Guirec except that it is much larger than the other two.

Inland, there is enough to keep one interested without burning up too much mileage or deserting the beaches for too long if it is fine. South of Lannion, up the valley of the Léguer, the charming little Renaissance Chapelle de Kerfons; the romantic, crumbling stone *donjon* and curtain-walls of the ruined Château de Tonquedec; the many-styled Château of Kergrist set in formal gardens; and the unique chapel of the Sept-Saints, built around a megalithic tomb, all lie a short distance off the road to Plouaret. If one cuts across country from here, through Lanmeur (church with a very early crypt), the church of St. Jean-du-Doigt is only some 8 kilometres (5 miles) further; it was built with the financial help of the Duchess Anne and treasures several important reliquaries, one containing part of St. John the Baptist's forefinger.

At the centre of this coast, on the Jaudy estuary, is **Tréguier**, capital of this region and home of Brittany's favourite saint, St. Yves, advocate of the poor, who lived in the late 13th century and was that most rare of beings, a just lawyer. He was buried in Tréguier's St. Tugdual Cathedral, as was the pious Duke Jean V, at whose instigation St. Vincent Ferrer was summoned to the Morbihan; their tombs were destroyed during the Revolution and replaced by new ones, but the lovely flamboyant Gothic cloister survives.

Further east, just south of Paimpol, celebrated in Pierre Loti's *Pêcheurs d'Islande*, are the melancholy, tree-shaded ruins of the Abbaye de Beauport, founded in the 13th century by monks from La Lucerne. About 14 kilometres (9 miles) further south the chapel of Kermaria has some unusual but rather deteriorated 15th-century frescoes. Further south still, the little chapel at Châtelaudren also has some badly damaged paintings, this time on wooden panels; while even further south is **Quintin**, a quiet old town with a restored castle, the remains of some ramparts, and a 19th-century basilica. Outside it, the Château de Robien stands just off the road to Corlay, where there are the remains of a Rohan castle; and all around are miles of strangely empty countryside, half-lost pools and streams, hamlets with chapels that only come to life once a year on their 'pardon' days; beautiful, overgrown byways occasionally marked by a menhir or wayside cross—and one returns to the coast by way of Guingamp, perhaps taking in Pontrieux and the beautifully sited castle of La Roche-Jagu, just north of it, on the way. Or perhaps one leaves them for another day, or another visit; there are so many secret, half-lost places in Brittany that it would take a lifetime to do them all justice.

Breton Cuisine

Breton cuisine, apart from the famous *crêpes*, is based on the principal indigenous ingredients of fresh fish and shellfish, marvellous vegetables, the meat of the young animals that graze its salt-meadows, local wines like Muscadet and Gros Plant, and cider. Cream and butter are also used liberally, as in these two basic Breton sauces, one hot and the other cold, both of which immediately impart a distinctive Breton flavour to many a familiar dish.

As well as being indebted to individual restaurants and chefs for help over some of the following recipes, I am once again thankful for facts culled from Simone Morand's book on Breton cookery, which is a companion volume to the Normandy one and an invaluable standby.

Notes on recipes and measurements see page 97

Beurre Blanc Nantais

Ingredients

Four good-sized shallots, minced

3 tablespoons wine vinegar

4–5 tablespoons white wine, court-bouillon (if the sauce is to go with poached fish) or water

salt

freshly ground black pepper

200–250 gr unsalted butter at room temperature

a few drops of lemon juice

2 dl commercially soured cream or crème fraîche (optional)

Method

Put the finely minced shallots into the smallest heavy pan available, add the vinegar and the wine, court-bouillon or water, and a little salt and pepper. Put over the lowest possible heat to simmer until the liquid has reduced by about half and the shallots have virtually melted away to a purée. Remove from heat but leave a saucepan of water gently simmering in its place in case it is necessary to warm the sauce up a little during the next stage, which is to beat in butter, piece by small piece, vigorously with a fork until the sauce achieves the consistency of heavy cream. The butter must be soft enough to blend with the liquid but must never melt entirely. At the very end, beat in a few drops of lemon juice and set the sauce somewhere where it will remain just tepid but not hot enough to become runny. The addition of the cream is recommended if the sauce is to accompany a dish already highly flavoured, such as *choucroute du pêcheur* (see p. 195); otherwise it is served, undiluted, with all manner of poached fish: pike, shad, seabream, grey mullet, bass, whiting, etc. Incidentally, a great deal of nonsense is talked about the difficulty of making this sauce properly: the crucial factor is not to let it get so hot that the butter melts.

Sauce Bretonne Froide

An admirable and quickly prepared mayonnaise substitute for salads and cold fish, made with butter instead of olive oil (which is not, of course, indigenous to Brittany).

Ingredients

2 large egg yolks
1 teaspoon pale French
  mustard or a good pinch
  of English mustard powder
salt
freshly ground black pepper
1 generous tablespoon finely
  chopped parsley, chives
  and chervil

a scant teaspoon finely
  chopped capers or gherkin
1 dl wine vinegar
75 gr melted butter, not hot
1 dl commercially soured
  cream

Method

With a fork, stir the mustard, salt, pepper, herbs, etc., into the egg yolks and gradually add the vinegar. When they are well blended, pour in the melted butter in a slow but steady stream, stirring until the sauce is thick and creamy. Keep it somewhere near the stove where it will remain just tepid, and at the last minute whisk in the cream, which will bring it down to the correct temperature for serving.

Incidentally, this sauce can also be served warm, without the addition of the cream, and is a delicious accompaniment to many varieties of fish if a tablespoonful of finely chopped sorrel is used instead of the capers or gherkins.

Potage aux Marrons de Redon

Ingredients

500 gr peeled chestnuts (if
    dried ones are used, they
    should have plenty of
    boiling water poured over
    them, be left to soak over-
    night, and then drained)
1 stick of celery

2 litres water
½ litre very hot milk
2½ dl commercially soured
    cream or crème fraîche
salt
pepper
knob of butter

Method

Cover the chestnuts with water, add the stick of celery and
boil for at least an hour, or until the chestnuts are very soft,
topping up with more boiling water from time to time if
necessary. Remove from the cooking liquid (disposing of the
celery stalk) and reduce them to a purée, either in a blender or
sieve, gradually adding the cooking liquid. Return to the stove
and add the almost boiling milk; simmer very gradually for
another half hour. Remove from the heat, season to taste, stir in
the cream and the butter, and keep the soup hot without
allowing it to boil until ready to serve.

Soupe aux Artichauts

Ingredients

200 gr onion, finely chopped
1 medium-sized leek, finely chopped
1 stick celery, finely chopped
250 gr butter
6 large cooked artichoke hearts (or 500 gr well-scrubbed Jerusalem artichokes)

1¼ litres light stock (chicken or veal)
salt
freshly ground black pepper
¼ litre milk
¼ litre cream
knob of butter
chopped parsley

Method

Gently sweat the onion, leek and celery in the butter in a covered saucepan until soft and golden. (If Jerusalem artichokes are used, slice them thinly and sweat them with the other vegetables; it may not be so pure-Breton a recipe but it is economical and extremely good.) Add the cooked artichoke hearts, diced, if the globe variety is used, noting the comment of the Breton housewife who gave me this recipe that 'One eats the leaves another day, of course, with a *sauce vinaigrette*, as an appetiser.' Shake the pan and allow the vegetables to continue softening together for another 10 minutes. Add the stock, simmer for half an hour, and then reduce to a fine purée through a sieve or in a blender—straining through a sieve in either case, if Jerusalem artichokes have been used, to remove the bits of skin. Add the milk and the cream, season to taste, and re-heat almost to boiling point. At the last moment, stir in a knob of butter and serve with a very little sprinkling of chopped parsley to emphasise its lovely pale green colour.

Cotriade

Basically, a fish soup: the Breton equivalent of *bouillabaisse* or *bourride*, and seldom made the same way twice, even by the same cook, since what goes into it depends very much on what is available from the fishmonger's that day. It is also very much a matter of taste whether it is served strained and smooth, or with the pieces of fish left whole in it, and whether it contains tomatoes and tomato-paste or not; my own feeling is that both greatly enhance the colour as well as the flavour. This version is based on one demonstrated to me by M. Siena, then head chef of the Manoir de Kerliviou, near Morlaix; it is easy to make yet sophisticated enough for a dinner party—and, like all good *cotriades*, capable of being adapted according to what is available.

Ingredients

60 gr lard
2 large onions, chopped
3 or 4 tomatoes, chopped
2 celery stalks, chopped
3 garlic cloves, chopped
2 large potatoes, peeled and
　sliced
4 tablespoons tomato purée
1 litre water
1½–2 kg mixed fish (rock-
　fish, red gurnet, sea bream,
　whiting, eel, mackerel)
　cut into thick chunks

saffron
bouquet garni comprising
　2 or 3 bayleaves, thyme
　and a good-sized branch
　of fennel or dill
salt
cayenne pepper
1 litre dry white wine
croutons
grated cheese

Method

Melt the lard and add the onion, garlic, celery, thyme, bayleaves, parsley, fennel/dill, stir, and start to soften them. After a few minutes, add a pinch of saffron, and the potatoes, stir again, and then throw in the chunks of fish, heads and all, plus any extra heads or bones the fishmonger can be persuaded to part with. Add the tomato purée, stir well again, pour in the water and the wine and add a little salt and cayenne. Bring to the boil, cover, and simmer for 30–40 minutes. Remove from heat and strain bit by bit into another saucepan, using a conical *chinois* sieve and pressing the fish chunks down hard, to extract the maximum flavour from them. Re-heat gently, correct the seasoning, and serve topped with garlic flavoured croutons and grated cheese. (To make the croutons, slice a not-too-fresh loaf of French bread, butter the slices, lay them on a buttered baking tray and put them in a hot oven for just long enough to make them crisp. Rub each one lightly with the cut side of half a garlic clove before floating them on the cotriade.)

Tourte aux Moules

Ingredients

1 pre-baked *pâte brisée* flan shell made of 350 gr flour
100 gr butter
30 gr lard
salt
4 tablespoons iced water.
For the filling: 1 knob of butter
3 medium-sized onions, finely chopped
3 medium-sized tomatoes cut into thick rounds

pinch of mustard powder
1 tablespoon tomato purée
3 litres mussels
150 gr shelled shrimps
glassful dry white wine
parsley stalks
2 dl heavy cream
2 large egg yolks
salt
cayenne pepper

Method (1)

Make the pâte brisée by rubbing the fats, cut into small bits, into the combined flour and salt. Add the water and turn the mixture with a knife blade until all the water is absorbed (adding more if necessary). Form the dough into a rough ball, turn it out on to a lightly floured board and push together with the heel of one hand for a few seconds until it becomes a smooth ball. Wrap in waxed paper and leave to rest in a cool place for at least an hour, after which roll it out to the necessary size (it should be about ½ cm thick) and line a 25 cm flan tin with it, leaving enough overhanging pastry to double back on itself, after damping slightly, to make a nice thick rim. Prick the base with a fork, cover with dry bread crusts, or with greaseproof paper on which you have sprinkled a handful of dried beans, and bake at 195°C (400°F, or just over gas mark 5) for 15 minutes before removing the bread crusts, or beans and paper, and baking for 10 minutes more.

Method (2)

While the pastry is resting, prepare the filling by softening the chopped onions in butter in a small saucepan, and stirring in the mustard and tomato purée when half done. In a frying pan, gently warm the tomato rounds in a little more butter; they should be soft but nowhere near fried. Put the wine and parsley stalks into a large pan, add the well-cleaned, scraped and scrubbed mussels; cover, and shake for 8–9 minutes over high heat, or until the mussels open their shells and are cooked. Transfer them on to a cloth and remove them from their shells. Line the pastry-case with a layer of onions, followed by a layer of tomato rounds, followed by the cooked mussels and finally the shrimps. Blend the cream and the egg yolks; gently re-heat in a small pan the strained liquid in which the mussels were cooked, and then stir in the egg and cream mixture. Season well, pour over the seafood, and bake for 35–40 minutes at 190°C (375°F, or gas mark 5) until firm and golden. The *tourte* can be topped with grated cheese for the last 10 minutes of cooking. Serve with plenty of green salad.

Moules à la Crème

Ingredients

3 litres mussels, scrubbed, scraped and washed
1 medium onion or 3 shallots, finely chopped
3 dl dry white wine
bouquet garni of parsley stalks, bayleaf and a sprig of thyme

300 dl crème fraîche
small knob of butter
pepper
chopped parsley

Method

Soften the onion or shallots in the butter for a few minutes in a large saucepan; add the bouquet garni and then the mussels. Pepper lightly, and pour the wine over them. Cover and shake over high heat for a few moments until the shells open and the mussels are cooked, and then transfer them with a perforated spoon, shells and all, to a large heated serving dish and put in a low oven to keep warm. Remove the bouquet garni from the cooking liquid and quickly stir in the cream, heating almost to boiling point. Pour the liquid over the mussels and serve immediately, helping them into individual soup plates, with plenty of fresh French bread for sopping up the sauce, as well as a spare dish in which to throw the empty mussel shells.

Maquereaux à la Quimperoise

Ingredients

court-bouillon comprising
2 litres water, 3 dl wine
vinegar, 2 tablespoons
cooking salt, 12 pepper-
corns, 1 sliced carrot, 1 or
2 sliced onions, parsley and
bayleaf
3 large mackerel or 6
medium-sized ones
2 egg yolks

1 teaspoon pale French
mustard or a pinch of
mustard powder
75 gr butter, melted but not
hot
dash of vinegar
salt
freshly ground black pepper
1 tablespoon finely chopped
parsley, chives and chervil

Method

Combine the court-bouillon ingredients, cover, and cook gently for about an hour. Leave to cool, strain, and pour over the mackerel in a pan broad enough to take them lying side by side, but not so large as to leave more than a hint of fish above the level of the liquid. Cover and bring gently to the merest simmer so that the surface of the liquid just shivers, until the fish are cooked. Leave to cool slightly in the court-bouillon and, when cool enough to handle, remove them gently, skin and fillet them, and arrange the fillets on a heated dish. Put in a low oven to warm up while making the sauce. This is done by much the same method as *sauce bretonne*, stirring together the egg yolks, mustard, vinegar, salt, pepper and chopped herbs, and then pouring in the melted butter. Continue stirring until creamy, pour over the fish fillets and leave in the oven a few more minutes until thoroughly hot.

Choucroute du Pêcheur

A highly unusual dish, which I found one day on the menu of the restaurant *Duchesse Anne* at St. Malo and have never seen elsewhere. Luckily, they were quite happy to divulge how to make it, and if one uses top quality tinned *choucroute* (sauerkraut), preferably the variety that is cooked in wine rather than vinegar, it is easily and quickly prepared.

Ingredients

1 kg wine-cooked (tinned) choucroute
1 glassful dry white wine
400 gr each of smoked haddock fillets and fresh turbot or brill fillets

200 gr smoked salmon (some delicatessens sell smoked-salmon scraps, left over after the best cuts have been taken off the fish, and these will do very well)
beurre blanc (see p. 185)

Method

Spread the choucroute in a layer at the bottom of a large shallow buttered baking dish and press the pieces of fish gently down into it in a pattern that both looks attractive and is conveniently spaced so that each person gets a piece of each type of fish. Moisten with the wine, cover with greaseproof paper, and put in a moderate oven until the choucroute is hot and the fish nicely poached. Meantime, make the beurre blanc, adding the optional 2 dl cream at the end, and pour it over the dish. Return to a low oven to heat gently and serve with tiny boiled new potatoes.

Poulet au Cidre

Ingredients

1 2-kg chicken, cut into 8
   serving pieces
200 gr streaky bacon, rinded
   and cut into matchstick-
   thin slivers
100 gr butter
2 shallots, finely chopped
salt

freshly ground black pepper
4 dl dry cider
¾ kg cooking apples,
   peeled and sliced
¾ kg tart dessert apples,
   peeled and sliced
2 dl heavy cream
half a lemon

Method

Melt half the butter in a heavy pan and soften the bacon
slivers in it until the fat runs. Season the chicken joints, first
with lemon juice and then salt and pepper, and *sauter* them
gently, turning until evenly golden. Add the chopped shallots
and, when they start to become transparent, pour over the
cider. Cover and simmer for 30–40 minutes, until well cooked
but not falling off the bone. Meantime, turn the apple slices in
the rest of the butter in another pan until they become soft and
buttery. When the chicken is done, remove the joints to a
serving dish and keep them warm in the oven. Skim the fat
from the cooking liquid, reduce over high heat for 5 minutes,
correct seasoning, pour in the cream and stir while re-heating.
Return the chicken pieces to the pan, together with the apple
slices, and shake gently together over a low heat for 5–10
minutes to combine thoroughly before returning to the
serving platter.

Epaule d' Agneau aux Haricots

Ingredients

500 gr white haricot beans, soaked overnight

1 shoulder of lamb, boned and rolled and tied

4 cloves garlic

1 large shallot stuck with 3 cloves

3 or 4 onions, chopped

2 tomatoes, peeled, seeded and chopped

1 tablespoon tomato paste

1 carrot

1 bouquet garni comprising parsley, thyme and bay-leaf

butter

salt

pepper

lemon juice

Method

Drain the beans and transfer them to a saucepan. Cover with fresh water, bring to boil and allow to stand for an hour, covered. Drain them again and add to them the shallot stuck with cloves, the carrot, two crushed garlic cloves, and a good tablespoon salt and the bouquet garni. Cover with boiling water, cover the pan and put to simmer for 1½–2 hours. Meantime, pre-heat the oven to 230°C (450°F or gas mark 8). If the boning and rolling of the lamb shoulder is done at home, sprinkle the inside with coarse salt and dot with slivers of garlic before rolling and tying; if it is done by the butcher, the garlic slivers must be inserted in the meat at intervals and the outside lightly salted halfway through the cooking. Sprinkle the lamb with a little lemon juice, rub with a little softened butter and roast in the hot oven for 25–30 minutes. Then turn the heat down (having lightly salted the joint, if necessary) to 160°C (325°F, gas mark 3) for another hour. While the meat and beans continue cooking melt a good knob of butter in another saucepan and gently soften the chopped onion in it, adding the tomato paste and the chopped fresh tomatoes after about 10 minutes. Drain the beans, reserving 3 dl of their cooking liquid, and add this to the onion and tomato mixture. Cover, and simmer briskly while removing from the beans the bouquet garni, carrot, cloves and shallot. Add the beans to the simmering liquid, shake well, cover and leave to continue simmering slowly. When the lamb is cooked (which should be almost coincidental with finishing the beans), remove it to a shallow serving dish, cut the strings away from it, and leave it to set at the bottom of the oven for 5–10 minutes. Turn the beans into the roasting pan to *déglacer* it, scraping the sides and bottom well to get up any bits stuck there, and shake it gently over the heat so that the meat juices combine well with the beans. Finally, tip the beans into the serving dish, surrounding the joint with them, and serve.

Vegetables

The Breton, with fields of artichokes and cauliflowers stretching away as far as the eye can see, cooks them in a wide variety of ways. Especially in the case of the artichoke, which to us is something of a luxury and normally either eaten hot with melted butter or cold with sauce vinaigrette, these seem superfluous. But a purée of dried haricot beans, which is a typically Breton dish, can make a pleasant change from mashed potato and is easy to do: having soaked the dried beans overnight and (as in the previous recipe) cooked them for two hours or more, flavoured with salt, an onion stuck with cloves, and a carrot, they are then rubbed through a sieve and whipped up with cream and butter before re-heating. Similarly, the following cauliflower dish makes a slightly unusual addition to a summer luncheon:

Choufleur à la St. Malo

Ingredients

1 fine firm cauliflower
1½ kg potatoes
1 good fistful of chives

300 gr shrimps, cooked and
    peeled
sauce bretonne froide (see p. 187)

Method

Simmer the potatoes in their jackets until just soft, drain and leave to cool slightly. Meantime, cook the cauliflower in boiling salted water for only about ¾ normal cooking time, so that it remains slightly crisp; drain and cool it. When the potatoes are cool enough to handle, peel and slice them and dress them in vinaigrette sauce, mixed with plenty of snipped chives. When all the vegetables are quite cold, arrange the potato salad in a ring around the cauliflower, cover with the *sauce bretonne froide*, and decorate with the shrimps.

Crêpes

Possibly the best-known of Breton specialities, the crêpe is capable of enormous variation. Here is a basic recipe with just a few suggestions for adapting it.

Ingredients

¾ kg fine white wheat flour
¼ kg buckwheat flour
3 large eggs
pinch of salt

350 gr caster sugar
350 gr cooled melted butter
¾ litre water
½ litre milk

Method

Mix the flour, salt and sugar in a bowl and blend in the slightly beaten eggs to which some of the water has been added.

Gently stir in with a wire whisk the rest of the water, the milk, and the melted butter, and leave the batter to rest for an hour (or as long as is convenient). When ready to cook, lightly oil a large heavy frying pan or a non-stick one, and heat it until the air above it seems to shimmer. Give the batter a quick stir, pour a ladleful into the smoking pan and at the same time tilt and turn the pan swiftly, so that the batter covers the entire bottom. Turn with a wooden spatula almost immediately and cook the other side. If one is cooking a large batch of crêpes, transfer them one by one to a warm dish; they will stand re-heating very well and in fact deep-freeze well too, so that one can make a quantity at a time and use them as needed. Sweet crêpes, of which this is the basic recipe, can be buttered and folded up with a filling of sugar and cinnamon; honey; jam; grated apple flambé in Calvados; grated chocolate, and any number of different sweet things, and then put in the oven to re-heat briskly before serving; the basic recipe can also be altered with the addition of vanilla or rum or brandy. Savoury crêpes are made in basically the same way except that the sugar is omitted and the amount of buckwheat flour proportionately increased, and they can be filled with cheese, ham, chicken or any other left-overs, either incorporated into a béchamel sauce (as with cheese) or simply sprinkled over the buttered crêpe and put into the oven to heat quickly after filling and folding.

Index of Places

Index of People